Argyll's Atlantic Islands
The Sea Kingdom

THE NÀDAIR TRUST

'Few places have their stories so eloquently inscribed across the landscape as Scotland's Sea Kingdom.'

VISIT SCOTLAND (www.visitscottishheartlands.com/seakingdom)

FOREWORD

It has been my pleasure to be involved with Nàdair since its earliest days and it is great to have this opportunity to celebrate the Trust's achievements and congratulate the many organisations, communities and individuals who have contributed to its success. The two Nàdair programmes completed between 2000 and 2008 with funding from the Heritage Lottery Fund and many others are the best example of sustainable development that I am aware of in the UK. Not only have they brought together delivery of real environmental benefits with positive community and economic impacts, they have given a new pride to the islands. New community venues have been created, new materials for island schools produced, an iconic floating school to sail the seas between the islands launched, wildlife management and monitoring programmes implemented and, above all, new generations welcomed to appreciate the wealth of wildlife and human heritage that the islands offer to visitors and residents alike.

Alongside this, for eight years, people across the islands have been planning and managing complex projects, honing new skills and building confidence. At each AGM, I have listened in awe as project achievements were presented and discussed with skill, determination and fervour. That delicious taste of success must be a great legacy of this programme. Key to this, was the rôle played by the staff of the Nàdair Trust who trained, cajoled and coaxed the projects through the complexities of planning, finding matched funding, management and reporting. So let's celebrate this legacy of real achievement!

Tricia Bradley RSPB SCOTLAND DIRECTOR, S&W SCOTLAND
FIRST CHAIR OF THE NÀDAIR TRUST
BOARD MEMBER OF THE NÀDAIR TRUST

June 2008

'Without Nàdair, small groups like us would never have been able to draw down the money to allow this sort of project to continue. As a model for allowing the penetration of Lottery funding into smaller community groups it is excellent.'

DR JOHN HOLLIDAY, AN IODHLANN, ISLE OF TIREE

INTRODUCTION

The Nàdair Trust was established in 2000 by a group of six founding partner organisations: the Royal Society for the Protection of Birds, VisitScotland (formerly AILLST), Argyll and the Islands Enterprise, Argyll and Bute Council, Historic Scotland and Scottish Natural Heritage. The name Nàdair means 'nature' in Gaelic and encompasses the idea of the land, people and wildlife of the Argyll Islands as an interdependent whole.

The inspiration for the Trust came from a growing recognition that, while Argyll's Atlantic Islands could boast some of the finest scenery, richest history and most spectacular wildlife in Britain, the islanders, who were the chief custodians of this resource, had received little or no support in their efforts to safeguard their heritage, or develop viable communities.

At the turn of the millennium 'sustainability' did not trip off the tongue as an aspiration quite as readily as it does now, nonetheless it was the key focus of the Nàdair Trust, expressed in an ambition to work with heritage in a way that not only conserved it, but regenerated fragile isolated communities, bringing economic, educational and social benefits.

Working with a range of community groups and specialist organisations, Nàdair's first programme of 28 heritage and sustainable development projects was launched in 2000, followed by a second round of 38 projects from 2005 to 2008.

Major funding support for the Nàdair programmes came from the Heritage Lottery Fund, with additional assistance from a wide range of statutory bodies and charitable trusts, as well as cash and in-kind contributions from partner organisations and the island communities.

THIS BOOK AND FILM

This book and the accompanying film paint a portrait of the people, the places and the projects that contributed to the Nàdair programmes. The text represents one individual's personal journey and observations, in this case those of Eleanor Garty who spent four years working for the Trust. The film was made over the course of two seasons by islander Andy Crabb, with Simon MacEachran who also took the photographs for the booklet. Not all of the projects could be represented within the film, so a selection was made in an attempt to demonstrate the range of activities involved, while giving a flavour of each island.

Together the booklet and film provide what is inevitably an incomplete account of an endeavour that involved hundreds of people and a vast array of natural, cultural and built heritage over a period of eight years. It is hoped that they convey a sense of what there is to value in these special islands and how much can be achieved through celebrating and nurturing that resource.

Lismore

'Lismore is an island where each ruin, each knoll carries some tale, some secret tradition unique to that spot; even evidence of cultivation is in itself a memorial to some long departed ploughman and other agricultural system.'

DONALD M. BLACK, CHAIRMAN, COMANN EACHDRAIDH LIOS MÒR

Comann Eachdraidh Lios Mòr / Lismore Historical Society, is a group of islanders who recognise their island's heritage as its most important resource; both for community identity and as a base for economic development. The result of their vision has been a remarkable achievement – **Ionad Naomh Moluag** / Saint Moluag Centre – a museum of Lismore's rich Gaelic heritage and a hub for community life.

Today I am standing on the crest of the island overlooking the museum, which nestles comfortably next to **Tigh Iseabail Dhaidh**, a little cottar's cottage, restored by the islanders to its 19th century appearance. The backdrop is spectacular; Ben Sgulaird and the twin horns of Ben Cruachan on the mainland, the great bulk of Ben Nevis to the north, Morvern to the west and, towards the open sea, the Isle of Mull.

Annie-the-Post arrives and a woman comes out of the cottage door to meet her. There's a pair of white bloomers flapping energetically on the washing line and a crop of pale green flax stems bending in the wind. If it wasn't for the shiny red post bus and the brand new museum building next door, it would be easy to imagine that a rare letter home was arriving from an emigrant in America, or a daughter in service in Glasgow.

'Being able to help…has probably been the most rewarding job I've ever had'

TONY PERKINS

The red letter occasion today is the first shoot for the Sea Kingdom film and the first leg of my tour around the islands of Argyll to see more than sixty Nàdair Trust projects. Andy and Simon the filmmaker and photographer team, are feeling their way, testing out some new equipment and adjusting to the idiosyncrasies of island-based filming. We had thought we were going to meet the whole committee of the Comann Eachdraidh today, but most members turn out to be either at the sheep sales or a funeral; this is not a sign of disinterest, merely an indication of the proper order of life (and death) on the island and perhaps just a little reticence towards the idea of performing to a camera.

We do, however, have the central figure from the project with us. Tony Perkins has put eight years of his life (not to mention a considerable proportion of his family's) into turning Comann Eachdraidh's vision into the solid reality that we can see across the field. It has been a monumental task, which he has undertaken with charm, diplomacy and a talent for inspiring others to contribute – he is such a genuinely delightful man that it is impossible to resist!

Tony is gesticulating in the air as he speaks; the pearly damp air gathers an ethereal glow about his cropped silvery hair. If it wasn't for his glasses, he would have just the same engagingly impish look as his young son Eoghan, who has waited patiently through hours of project meetings in his dad's company.

Tony is explaining the history of the project, how Comann Eachdraidh first set up an archive, based in the vacant schoolteacher's house and in 2002, with the gift of a plot of land from local farmer Duncan Macgregor, they embarked on rebuilding the ruined cottar's house.

'Many of us have done things we never dreamt we would have done.'

DONALD BLACK

'The visitors enjoy looking round at how people lived without any of the mod cons that people have nowadays.'

MARGARET MACDONALD

Tigh Iseabail Dhaidh, named after its last occupant, was an immediate success when it opened its doors to the public, gaining a prestigious tourism award in the first year and attracting a stream of walkers and cyclists to make the short journey over to Lismore on the ferry. Successful as it was, however, the members of the Comann Eachdraidh moved on swiftly to realize their ambition to give their archive and collection a permanent home and provide the island with much needed facilities – a café, a library, computers, a meeting room and an outlet for local crafts and produce (not to mention public toilets!).

At over half a million pounds, the level of funding needed for the new building was never going to be easy to achieve, but the charm and hospitality of the Liosaich played a pivotal role in bringing it in. Visitors to the project (whether or not they came bearing gifts) would be met by a welcoming committee after the short crossing from Port Appin and be given a guided tour of the island, rain or shine. With Chairman Donald Black as a guide, the passing landscape would come alive. Storytelling is woven into Donald's everyday conversation and happenings of the 1880's are recounted alongside events from last week – the neighbours who never spoke because of some long forgotten fall-out in a previous generation but nonetheless turned up each year to help with each other's harvest – the lady visitor from Australia who was horrified to discover that she was descended from an infamous 'clearing' landowner.*

Having 'done' the island sights – the broch at Tirfuir, the Bishop's palace at Achinduin, the pretty row of lime workers' cottages at Port Ramsay and, of course, Tigh Iseabail Dhaidh, the visiting party would reach the school house, where Margaret MacDonald, Secretary of the Comann Eachdraidh, would be waiting armed with pots of tea and bowls of soup and a groaning table of home baking provided by fellow committee members. Personally, I am convinced that it was the clootie dumpling that tipped the balance in favour of funding on a number of occasions.

Margaret is at the Museum today. Andy and Simon want to interview her for the film, so I stand in at the reception desk in the beautiful new building. Shauna Cameron, the project architect, steered the building through several permutations dictated by budget, planning requirements and the vision of the islanders, to create a hugely satisfying and pleasingly simple structure. On the outside it is clad with larch, which is already weathering to a soft grey; a glass gable and a balcony face forward giving the café a view over the surrounding landscape. My favourite feature, the roof, is a gentle angle of green turf. Several times larger than the little croft house beside it, the museum does not dominate the space, but sits well on the land, the grass roof almost melting into the field behind it.

In a lull between new arrivals, I nip into the exhibition area for a look at the beautifully designed display. Catherine Gillies and Jennifer Baker are joint Museum Development officers and have put an immense amount of work into curating the collection of documents and artefacts, as well as creating this fascinating exhibition. A series of banners tell the story of the island – I spot a picture of Comann Eachdraidh committee member Archie MacColl – younger, but scarcely different, broadcasting seed from a sling at his waist. The text explains

the communal farming system as it would have been practised on the island prior to the 19th century – well before Archie's time, but no doubt his predecessors would have used the same skilful flick of the wrist to sow their crops.

> '*The infield was a system of rig and furrow used for crops. A rig would be ploughed, usually by four horses in a row. The rigs were sown in rotation – usually oats, barley, potatoes and other root crops.*'

IONAD NAOMH MOLUAG – EXHIBITION AREA, COMANN EACHDRAIDH LIOS MÒR

Margaret comes back to take over her post and I set off walking back to the ferry, with time for a detour down to Castle Coeffin on the western shore. The Viking prince, Coeffin, built his castle on this steep-sided knoll, where his sister, Beothail, died of a broken heart. Her spirit haunted the castle and did not rest until she was taken back across the sea to be buried beside her lost love in Norway.

Today the craggy silhouette looks peaceful against a sparkling sea and I for one don't want to leave this island. Less peaceful, though, are the activities of Glensanda Quarry across the water on Morvern, but it is every bit as much a part of the island's recent history as the Vikings are of its distant past. The quarry has for a number of years provided employment to islanders and Mrs. Yeoman, until recently its owner, was hugely supportive of the museum project, donating building materials and the use of the company barge.

Looking out over the shifting pattern of water, sky and rock, I think that all of the Nàdair projects have affected me in some way, well beyond the everyday involvement of my working life; but it is Lismore that has had the most profound effect. It was a large and complex project and closer at hand than some of the other islands – both factors which allowed me to become a little better acquainted with the people involved.

Seeing how this community works has given me clues to how the Nàdair projects have succeeded on island after island around the Sea Kingdom, each led by people who have to be innovative to survive and who know how to cooperate with their neighbours (even if they don't always agree!). Beyond this, there are two other things that they all have in common – a recognition of their island's heritage as a rich and precious resource and the daring to take on the risk of change.

Back at the ferry I meet up with Andy and Simon. The day's filming has gone well, but they are already planning to come back, timing their visit to coincide with the next 'Friday Fish and Chips' night – a new island tradition instituted by locals Gill and Davie since they took on the lease of the Lismore café at Ionad Naomh Moluag. Barring births, deaths, marriages and sheep sales, the Liosaich are sure to turn out in force for that event!

*For more Lismore stories see Donald's book 'Sgeul No Dhà as an Lios: A Tale or Two from Lismore' published by the University of Strathclyde Faculty of Education.

Isle of Mull

'Aon uair 's gun tig sibh a Mhuile – 's cinnteach gun till sibh a-rithist.'
'If you come to Mull the once – you will return again for sure.'

MULL & IONA: A WILDLIFE AND HERITAGE GUIDE – MULL AND IONA COMMUNITY TRUST

A day trip to Mull from Oban is feasible, but frustrating. This is a big island, the only one of the Hebrides to rise to a Munro (Ben More – The Big Mountain); to see it all in so short a time one would need to be riding one of the island's famous Sea Eagles. Earthbound, I will be navigating the narrow roads, which are high on the agenda of complaints for many Mull residents, with their frequent potholes and tidal surges of coach traffic coming in off the ferry. For those with time, or a bicycle, however, they hold an unparalleled charm.

My first destination today is Lochbuie, well off the beaten tourist route, over a twisty pass and then along Loch Spelve, a curious anvil shaped inlet from the sea, to Loch Uisg, where I take a guilty pleasure in the mauve *Rhododendron ponticum* glowing poisonously, like a beautiful, radioactive cloud under the ancient oakwood.

These islands are often characterised as tree-less and compared to the mainland they are indeed short on sylvan glades. Once you start to notice, though, there are pockets of woodland everywhere, wind sculpted fringes along the coast and slivers of ancient oak, ash and hazel woods clinging to the sides of steep ravines. As part of the Nàdair programme, the **Argyll Islands Native Woodland Project** has been raising the profile of these precious fragments, working with local communities and land managers to assess and prioritise suitable woodland expansion areas on Mull.

Arriving at the sheltered low-lying land that backs Lochbuie bay, the road skirts behind a boggy field, where a line of whitewashed stones marches towards a distant stone circle. The road peters out above the shore and I am astonished to find a green campervan, the exact match of my 'Valkyrie', parked gazing out to sea. I leave the two side by side, hoping that some small miracle of procreation might deliver me a shiny new model when I return.

Lochbuie is the ancestral seat of the Clan McLaine (as distinct form the McLeans of Duart up the road by Craignure). On the far side of the bay is an Iron Age dùn; it is not known if its inhabitants were of the same clan, but it was certainly plundered for building stone to make **Moy Castle**, the tower house that rises with apparent solidity between the trees.

As tastes leaned towards more comfort and less warfare, the castle was in its turn replaced by a more modern dwelling a short distance away. This house, now demoted to the status of an outbuilding, once hosted the famous literary travellers, Boswell and Johnson on their tour of the Western Isles in 1773. Johnson noted that *'Lochbuy has, like the other insular chieftans, quitted the castle that sheltered his ancestors and lives near it in a mansion not very spacious or splendid'*.

The present day Lochbuie House (1793) is, on the other hand, spacious and indeed rather splendid in a comfortable, friendly sort of way and as I approach up the drive I am met by its present owner, Jim Corbett, amidst a milling plethora of dogginess. In his journal Boswell described the laird 'Lochbuy' as *'a bluff, comely, noisy old gentleman, proud of his hereditary consequence and a very hearty and hospitable landlord ...'*. Jim deserves only the more flattering of these epithets, to which might be added 'charm' and 'shrewdness' for good measure.

'If one is lucky enough to live in a place like Lochbuie, one does have a moral responsibility to try and see that it doesn't fall down 'round your ears.'

JIM CORBETT

'One of the problems with ruins is water penetration...during the winter it rains constantly, for months on end.'

DUNCAN STRACHAN

*Mull Historical and Archaeological Society also delivered another Nàdair project, the Mull On Line Museum, which created a fantastic website (www.mull-historical-society.co.uk) – well worth a visit for information about everything to do with Mull's places, people and past.

Armed with one of his own beautifully crafted shepherd's crooks and a powerful torch, we set off to look at the conservation work in progress on Moy Castle.

A mediaeval tower house in one's garden is quite a responsibility. Jim's family have been propping things up and sticking bits back on for a couple of generations, but by the winter of 2005 it was looking as if the seaward gable might collapse with the first severe westerly storm. Mull Historical and Archaeological Society* had already applied for support for a consolidation project through Nàdair and, just in time, the necessary funding came through. My predecessor at the Trust, Dugie Bannatyne, liked to report Jim's reaction when he heard that that the project could go ahead: 'Good grief!' he exclaimed 'Now I believe in fairies!'

We clamber under the scaffolding to reach a small door leading into the darkness, taking care not to step into the well in the middle of the floor. The ceiling is barrel vaulted; lime-rinded, damp-dripping stones are canted in perfect alignment over our heads. It is this vaulting that makes Moy Castle unusual, not in itself, because it was a common technique, but because the room above it is also vaulted, with the arch running at right angles to the one we stand beneath. This makes an exceedingly strong construction and it is in fact the later additions to the upper parts of the building that are less secure and in need of the most urgent repair work.

The narrow flight of stairs winds up inside the thick wall, passing a smaller room, where Jim says that corpses used to be laid out, and into the main chamber. In one corner a doorway leads into a dark menacing space, where a hole in the floor reveals a bottle dungeon, half filled with cold, inky water.

I am rather glad that Jim is a less 'rough and haughty' laird than his predecessor. Boswell recounts: *'After breakfast we surveyed the old castle, in the pit or dungeon of which Lochbuy had some years before taken upon him to imprison several persons, and though he had been fined a considerable sum by the Court of Justiciary he was … little affected by it.'*

In the upper works of the castle we find the contractor, Duncan Strachan, a man to whom I would entrust the reconstruction of the Taj Mahal should it ever collapse. Duncan is a natural teacher and explains the work with great clarity and endless patience. He points out areas of new pinning, the small stones that fill the spaces between larger blocks, showing how the new stones stand proud from the lime mortar, so that it is easy to distinguish which areas are original – with the stones flush against the mortar – and which areas are repairs. This technique stems from the approach of 'conservation, not restoration', which makes only the interventions necessary to preserve the fabric and ensures that the present day work does not masquerade as original. These masons think of their work in terms of centuries and are mindful of the evidence they contribute to the archaeological record of the future.

Ben Weaser shows us the seaward gable, now secure after weeks of painstaking and, frankly, dangerous work. Ben is a Nàdair veteran, having worked on the Priory on Oronsay; he is also the only Argyll-bred member of the team, coming from Kilmelford not far away across the water on the mainland.

'Buildings are important... once they are gone, they're gone forever.'

<small>MARTIN HADLINGTON</small>

It is from that direction that we see Martin Hadlington, architect and designer of the castle's conservation scheme arriving in his sea kayak. Though tall and red bearded, Martin does not strike one immediately as the iron-man type; he has none of the alpha male bullishness and instead radiates goodwill and diplomacy. This, though, is a man who competes in the gruelling Hebridean Challenge each year and who, in his professional life, will hold out tenaciously against all regulation, be it from state bodies or funders, if he feels it will compromise the quality of his work. He is passionate about conservation of old buildings and endlessly optimistic in the face of the setbacks and delays that inevitably dog projects of this type.

Before we clamber back down the castle, Jim points out the spot where a plaque inscribed with the 'Curse of Moy' was mounted during the filming of the 1945 Powell and Pressbuger film 'I Know Where I'm Going'. In the film a young woman comes to Mull to join her rich industrialist fiancé, filled with determination to make a good match. Once on the island she succumbs instead to the charms of the romantic, cursed and not so wealthy Laird of Kiloran. The landscape of Mull appears curiously disjointed in the film, as if it has been taken apart and reassembled without much reference to its original geography. Some of these liberties are cinematographic, but others originated with Jim's grandmother, who, fearing an unwelcome level of interest in her home, dictated that while the castle could be used, all the surrounding shots had to be made elsewhere. The film has now achieved a measure of cult status and, rather ironically given the late Mrs. Corbett's feelings, a convention of 'IKWIG' enthusiasts came to visit Moy in 2005 to celebrate the film's 60th anniversary.

Taking a different route out of the castle, Jim and I climb over the ramparts and down the ladders through the scaffolding. Although this has been a major piece of work, the Nàdair project will only deal with the most unstable parts of the castle and, until the fairies deliver the next pot of gold, the building will not be open for general access. All visitors may see the exterior and its beautiful setting, but only those who have made prior appointment will be able to see the interior. I can't help but hope that visitor numbers to this lovely spot remain at a level where Jim can still take time away from the farm to lead his very personal guided tours and maintain Lochbuie's reputation for hearty hospitality.

Leaving Lochbuie, after refuelling with tea and signing the visitors' book, I make my way back to the 'main' road and head west to the Ross of Mull, seen by many passing travellers at the springboard for Iona, but in itself an area rich in natural beauty and riddled with folklore, legend and social history, much of which has been meticulously collected by the Ross of Mull Historical Centre (ROMHC) in Bunessan.

When I first visited Amber Knight, project officer for ROMHC's initial Nàdair project – **Discover the Ross** – the Centre was housed in a distinctly damp, some might say mouldering, portacabin at the side of the road. From these premises Amber and a team of volunteers created a network of seven way-marked routes around the Ross, accompanied by detailed and beautifully illustrated guidebooks. Just for today, Amber has left her brother's shellfish business in the lurch and is going to walk the 'District of Kilvickeon' route with me.

Lochbuie – Mull

As always, she is full of enthusiasm as she strides down the track, reddish blond hair flying in the wind.

> *'The area of Kilvickeon is one of rugged beauty with stunning sea views … The area boasts tales of heroism and horror, of great loss and sacrifice and of war.'*
>
> DISCOVER THE ROSS – ROSS OF MULL HISTORICAL CENTRE / IONAD EACHDRAIDH AN ROIS MHUILICH

After a small diversion to look at the ruins of the 13th century Kilvickeon Chapel, we head across the springy moor towards the coastline and the prominent Iron Age Fort, Dùn a' Gheàrd perched on the cliffs above Port Bheathain, or as it is sometimes known, the Bay of Thumbs.

> *Clann 'ill athain luchd nan geur-lainn*
> *Chir iad trued air Clann 'ic Phi*
> *Ann Port Bheathain na bha beò dhiubh*
> *Bha na h-òrdagan nan dhith*
>
> *The Clan MacLean, people of the sharp swords*
> *Were in dispute with the Clan MacPhee*
> *In the Bay of Beathain, those who were left alive*
> *Were left without their thumbs*
>
> JOHN CAMPBELL OF TOASLIN 1905–1999 – ROMHC

The battle of the Bay of Thumbs was the culmination of a long history of bloody murders and insults to clan honour. On this occasion the MacPhees had come to Mull to steal cattle, but were surprised by a MacLean ambush. As they dragged their boats into the surf to flee, their pursuers waded in after and chopped off their enemies' thumbs as they tried to man the oars.

Amber and I now head east past Scoor House, home of famous fighting men of more recent times, and take the track to the abandoned township of Shiaba. Above us a Golden Eagle (Iolaire Bhuidhe) spirals – I've heard the Sea Eagle described as a 'flying door' – it is rather bigger than the Golden – but even this bird looks capable of a one-winged total eclipse if it flies across the sun.

The story of Shiaba encapsulates the sadness and loss of clearance and emigration which is a recurring theme around the Ross of Mull. The Ross suffered particularly harsh treatment at the hands of the notorious Factor Mòr or Big Factor, as the Duke of Argyll's Chamberlain, John Campbell, was known. Hunger and overcrowding were certainly issues in 19th century Scotland, particularly following the potato famine, but the creation of larger, more profitable sheep farms was a key motivator for clearing tenants from their crofts.

Amber is visibly moved by the plight of the people who left this beautiful, deserted spot. She reads out a petition sent to the Duke of Argyll by crofters who did not want to leave their land.

'… the petitioners were lately warned to flit and remove from their respective possessions although they were not in arrears of rent, but on the contrary have paid the same regularly, though they had families to support – numbering, including cottars, upward of one hundred persons … the petitioners are in a dilemma and in a state of uncertainty of what is to be done with them.'

LETTER TO THE DUKE OF ARGYLL FROM THE TENANTS OF SHIABA – ROMHC

Maybe it's just the stiff, bog myrtle scented breeze coming in from the sea, but I find that my eyes prickle as I imagine the sad procession leaving Shiaba. Their petition did not prevail and some headed to other settlements on the Ross, while others made the journey to the New World. The wound is still felt in these communities, although these days it is more symbolic than painful. I recall with some amusement a visit to Islay, John Campbell's final resting place, when Amber and Janet MacDonald, another feisty Muileach, danced a Highland Fling with much satisfaction on the Factor Mòr's grave.

Back at Bunessan, Amber swaps her muddy black wellies for clean white ones and heads down to the pier to supervise the catch coming in, while I make my way to the new Ross of Mull Historical Centre, which will soon move from the portacabin to the much more picturesque setting of **Tigh an Rois,** a converted cottage next to the old Bunessan Mill.

Rosie Burgess, the Chair of the Centre greets me, carrying a very welcome picnic basket and we sit out on the grass with staff members Fiona Shannon and Andrea Sayers. Work on the cottage is still in progress, but we can peek inside, while Fiona, who has been managing the project, describes the layout. There will be an exhibition area and an archive room, which will allow the Centre's huge array of documents, pictures, artefacts and oral history recordings to be safeguarded and displayed. This won't just be a memorial to the past though; already local people are dropping in regularly for a chat and the Centre organises social events, like ceilidhs and guided walks, to involve islanders and visitors in local culture and traditions.

Having packed in as much as possible in one day on Mull (and quite a few of Rosie's sandwiches), I head off down to the tip of the Ross to catch the sun setting over the sacred Isle of Iona. My eldest daughter is named after this holy isle and despite the numbers of tourists that cross to visit it every day, it remains a very special place. At Fionnaphort I pop into the village shop for supplies and a chat with its owner, Sandy Brunton. I'm quite surprised to find him at the counter exchanging sweeties for a fistful of coins from a diminutive customer; Sandy is an active member of his community and spends a great deal of his valuable time away from home attending meetings. Equally at ease in the company of politicians and small boys, he is quizzing his customer about the fishing bait that he used today. Sandy has his head characteristically cocked to one side, treating the boy's answers with utmost seriousness and interjecting his own wry insights from time to time, just as I have seen him doing in committee meetings of the Scottish Islands Federation, The Development Trusts Association and no doubt at meetings of the Mull and Iona Community Trust (MICT), which he Chairs.

MICT is a grassroots powerhouse on Mull, thanks to the efforts of Sandy, his committee and their energetic Development Manager, James Hilder, whom I will be seeing in Tobermory tomorrow. They have been involved in a range of projects from setting up a Community Business Resource Centre to running the annual Taste of Mull & Iona Food Festival. As part of the Nàdair programme, MICT developed the **Mull & Iona Wildlife and Heritage Trail** and when I set out for Tobermory the following morning I have my own battered copy of the trail leaflet ready to guide me on the scenic route up the West side of Mull.

Mull is an island which receives a fair share of visitors, but many, on the way to lovely Iona Abbey, or the colourful town of Tobermory, pass by scores of other places of beauty and interest. The Wildlife & Heritage Trail uncovers some of these other 'not to be missed' sites, such as the spectacular Eas Fors waterfall, which plunges 30m from the cliffs into the sea, and the unusual pencil-spired church in the village of Dervaig.

My first stop along the trail is Balmeanach, after a breathtaking section of road, crossing the neck of the Ardmeanach peninsula and swooping back down to the coast. It is possible to reach MacKinnon's cave from here, previously used by an Abbot of Iona as a retreat, but I give it a miss today as the tide is creeping in and I don't relish the possibility of being trapped inside.

Travelling on, I pass what must surely be the only piece of Australian territory in the Hebrides, the mausoleum of Sir Lachlan MacQuarrie the 'Father of Australia'. Here my route heads east, across the narrow neck of Mull to pretty Salen, where swans float majestically in the bay against the backdrop of picturesquely disintegrating boats and the equally decrepit but enchanting outline of Aros Castle. From here it is a short drive to Tobermory, famed as the location for the children's television series 'Balamory', as well as for its colourful row of seafront shops and houses.

Silurian, the research and survey vessel of the **Hebridean Whale and Dolphin Trust** (HWDT) is at home, moored alongside the pontoons. In the HWDT visitor centre fluffy dolphins and porpoise pencil sets vie for attention with a range of fascinating interpretative materials. I can't resist putting on the headphones for a quick listen to the weird conversational gambits of a school of Minke whales. Staff Member Andrew Livingston ushers me into a room at the back where I am welcomed like a member of the family by Barbara Weir, who rather charmingly addresses me, and everyone else, as 'dear'. Barbara turns her dark Celtic-blue eyes on me with an expression of kindly worry; she is the administrative lynchpin of the organisation and has the unenviable job of keeping its finances afloat. Silurian, while a flagship in every sense of the word, has a tendency to soak up money and Barbara spends a great deal of her time juggling cashflows and grant claims to make it all work.

Cally Fleming, the executive director, also tends to have a slightly abstracted air; no wonder, given the vast range of research projects and educational initiatives the Trust delivers, but like Barbara she has a ready smile and when she talks about the Trust's work her dedication is palpable. Today she is describing the range of species seen on a recent seven-day survey, counting them off on her long, mobile fingers; 'harbour porpoise, minke whale, bottlenose dolphin, basking sharks and *two* killer whales west of Canna.' Information from the surveys is used to investigate distribution and to identify key habitats in the region for different species. By comparing sightings data over recent years, important areas for cetaceans have been identified and changes in distribution monitored. Sightings information comes from a range of sources, from volunteer-manned trips on the *Silurian*, from land based sightings at key points such as the Ardnamurchan peninsula and from boat operators and sailors around the Hebridean waters. To encourage involvement from the general public, HWDT runs awareness-raising and identification sessions, generating a veritable army of cetacean spotters.

When I first came across HWDT, I had recently returned from a spell in the United States, where I had watched in vain from Pacific Northwest islands to catch a glimpse of a migrating whale. Imagine my shock to discover that the waters of my homeland had been positively bristling with marine mammals all along; in fact it is fair to say that with their variety of birds, beasts and things that lurk in the sea, the Hebrides offer one of the finest wildlife watching experiences in Europe.

To make sure that the next generation does not grow up as ignorant as I did, HWDT operates a floating classroom from *Silurian* during term time. The vessel sails from island to island inviting schoolchildren aboard to learn about their marine heritage. Just in case the real thing proves elusive on the day, education staff are well equipped with a range of props, including a life-sized inflatable whale and dolphin! Idle moments on the ferry pier at Craignure have also been appropriated for sealife education, this time by another Nàdair project, **Wildlife from the Boat** run by Argyll and Bute Council, which placed a series of information boards down the length of the covered pedestrian waiting area.

Just for me, today there are five lively bottlenose dolphins out in the bay. Trust staff appear and set off in a RIB to photograph them for identification purposes; while the rest of Tobermory stops to watch the fun. Even James Hilder of Mull and Iona Community Trust suspends his usual state of perpetual motion as he dashes out of his office. He's just been moving goods into the MICT charity shop and sports a rather holey t-shirt and jeans (maybe rejects from the consignment?), but slung over his shoulder is an immaculate suit ready to be worn for this afternoon's conference address on 'Enterprising Communities'. James is a charismatic individual; his energy creates tidal waves which reach many places far from the shores of Mull, but this island and what can be done to make it a better, more livable place, is at the top of his priority list.

Also on the street watching the dolphins is Janet MacDonald, coordinator of the **Community Gaelic** project, which aims to bring a flavour of Gaelic language and culture to Muilich, particularly to those who run businesses that bring them face to face with visitors. Knowing the basics of Gaelic creates a living link with the island's heritage and a means of communicating it to others. Perhaps the most evocative and most often encountered Gaelic words are place names; there are more purely Gaelic place names on Mull than any other island. Their

'We've got groups of children coming on board learning a little bit about the sea.'
DAVE HANNAH

meanings enrich the landscape by describing its colours and shapes and commemorating past events or usage : buidhe – yellow, dubh – black, scriadain – scree, rudha – a point, eilean – island, Taigh an Uillt – House of the River, Cnoc a' Bhuntàta – Hill of the Potatoes, Linne na Duais – Pool of the Prize. Janet and her team of native Mull Gaelic speakers have put all of this and more onto a CD, giving the local pronunciations – which may be quite different to, say, neighbouring Lismore's – of each word.

I am back on the road now, heading south towards the ferry at Craignure. Before I leave the island though, I have one more visit planned, to the ***Operation Easter – Sea Eagle Watch*** project. Dave Sexton of RSPB Scotland meets me at the Loch Frisa hide, a location made famous by the BBC 'Springwatch' programme when it came to film the island's best known 'returnees', the white tailed or sea eagles. There are no fledglings to watch this year; after six successful breeding seasons on Mull, Skye and Frisa lost their chicks this spring, an event recorded by Dave in an article called 'White Tail: Black Day' which evokes the enormous sense of disappointment felt by all those who had watched over the eagle pair during the incubation period:

'As we watched, first Skye then a few seconds later, Frisa flew purposefully out from the direction of the nest and flapped slow and hard down the loch, over Ledmore and on and on into the distance. I knew immediately that something wasn't right. But we kept watching; hoping beyond hope that one of them would soar round in a big arc and return to the nest. But they just kept going. It could only mean one thing. Neither Skye nor Frisa would allow eggs or newly hatched chicks to remain uncovered in these conditions.

Slithering down the bank through the moss and broken branches of the thick forest, down to the exposed roots of the tree, there were the egg shells. Then my eye caught sight of something else. Something white; a strange shape; was it bits of prey that had fallen off the nest too? And there was another one a few feet away. All at once, as the haunting, echoing calls of Skye and Frisa cried out from above us, the truth, the identity of the downy white lifeless items at my feet hit me with a mixture of disbelief and panic.'

FROM 'WHITE TAIL: BLACK DAY' BY DAVE SEXTON
(http//:blogs.rspb.org.uk/mulleagles)

Today, without Dave to point me in the right direction, I would not have spotted Skye hunched on what appears to be a standing stone on the other side of the loch. The great bird looks like he is mourning, but Dave tells me that the pair has remained on territory since the sad event and that they are behaving normally. Through the 'scope there is an element of the comic about Skye, with his cartoonish banana beak; but when he lifts heavily into the air and stretches out his vast wingspan, there is majesty in his flight. I make a wish on the trajectory of his flight: 'next year, next time, may your chicks thrive and fledge and grow to be as magnificent as you are'.

Erne Flight

Coll

PROJECTS

Coastal Archaeology (inter island)

Discover Coll Leaflet

*Wild Flowers of Coll & Tiree
and an Index to the Coll Magazine*

Totronald Reserve

Assessment of Predation on Breeding Waders

Wildlife for All (inter island)

Schools Heritage (inter island)

'Col for my money!'

'A JOURNEY TO THE WESTERN ISLES OF SCOTLAND', SAMUEL JOHNSON

*'More and more is unfolding as we go along …
It's self driven, it's a grass roots operation.'*

JIM HILL

There is a track over the bog to Fiskary now. The new owner has been putting it in since Jim Hill sold the croft house and built himself a bright little cottage in the next cove. Approaching Jim's new home, the track gives way to an elegant boardwalk contouring up and around the hummocky ground.

As an engineer who, amongst other things, worked on the Pompidou Centre in Paris, it is no surprise to see that Jim has conjured up a new house since my last visit; but it is his more recently acquired field of expertise, archaeology, that brings me back to Fiskary.

Typical of the Hebridean coastlines, this stretch of Coll's shore is littered with the evidence of past lives, layer upon layer, from the hunter gatherers of the Mesolithic period, to the crofters of the last century. The three year **Coastal Archaeology** project, led by the SCAPE Trust *(Scottish Coastal Archaeology and the Problem of Erosion)* and the Centre for Environmental History and Policy at St. Andrews University, brought in volunteers like Jim to survey and monitor the coastlines of Coll, Tiree and Islay and feed information about archaeology, geomorphology and erosion risk into a central database.

Checked shirt flapping in the wind and yellow wellies firmly planted on the rocks, Jim gestures enthusiastically as he describes his archaeological realm. He takes a gleeful pleasure in challenging some of the 'givens' of academia and he has a talent for wrapping physical evidence and his own deeply pondered theories into fresh and fascinating narratives.

It takes us most of the afternoon to walk maybe a mile and a half of shoreline; there is so much to see. Jim populates the coast with prehistoric shellfish gatherers, skilful Viking oarsmen and peaceful, farming monks. All along the rocky edges above the sea are fist-sized basins cut into the rock, perhaps to hold offerings to the sea gods, or maybe for grinding bait. Jim suspects that whatever their purpose, they were hugely important to the people who must have laboured long to shape them in the hard Lewisian gneiss. He tells me that they are not a Scottish peculiarity and are found in many places around the world.

We stand at the end of a long trench cut into the land from the sea and Jim invites me to guess what it is. 'Fish trap?' I hazard – but it turns out that we are standing where the prow of a Viking longboat would have rested, secure in its specially cut 'boat noost' which allowed easy hauling up the shore, safe holding and, perhaps even more important, a quick and easy launching point for a pirate ship to dart out from.

Eventually I take my leave of Jim and make my way back across the bog, head full of ideas and pictures. Back on the tarmac road it isn't too far to Emma Grant's house, where a delicious confusion of babies, cakes and tea is happening in the garden. Emma, who masterminded the **Wild Flowers of Coll & Tiree** project could be slightly intimidating if she wasn't so warm and welcoming – a supreme multi-tasker, she seems to be chairing several committees at once, while one child swings on her long braid and another clamps limpet-like to her hip.

I have always liked the story of how Emma met her husband Pete MacKay: finding herself living on Coll, where there is only a limited pool of bachelors at a young woman's disposal, she set eyes on a handsome visitor one Show day. Encumbered with other people's bairns at the time, she introduced herself with the words 'They're not mine!'

Today, at least some of the bairns in the garden are Emma and Pete's and I watch them play, thinking what an idyllic existence young children have on these islands. When they are a little older they will have to leave Coll to board at the High School in Oban, an arrangement that can mean weeks at a time away from home. The introduction of a new Oban to Coll air service will soon allow more frequent visits home – but, unfortunately, not every weekend for every pupil, as the eight-seater plane cannot hold the entire (and growing) cohort of island students.

Neighbouring Tiree has a different situation; a larger population means that it can support its own high school. No doubt there are advantages, as well as disadvantages, in each island's educational circumstances – early acclimatisation to the outside world on the one hand and less disruption to family life on the other. I wonder if these contribute to the individuality of the two islands, which lie close physically, but seem culturally quite different.

It is also tempting to see the hand of feudalism in the character of the islands; most of Tiree is under crofts or tenanted farms owned by the Duke of Argyll, while Coll is now largely owner-occupied with relatively recent settlers (only a generation or three!). The original, rather brutal, reason for this is described in the **Discover Coll** leaflet, which was produced as part of the Nàdair programme:

> 'In 1841 Coll's population was over 1400, but by the turn of the century it had fallen to 432. This was largely due to the "land improvement" policy of John Lorne Stewart .... He swept aside fifty nine out of seventy traditional crofts in favour of large dairy units. Ayrshire cattle and Kintyre dairying folk were imported, and many of Coll's islanders were given 'assisted passages' to Canada, America, Australia and New Zealand.'

Presumably the Kintyre farmers were an adventurous lot if they were willing to take their chances on a small lump of rock so far from the fertile mainland. The leaflet goes on to describe the wide range of enterprises that have been trialled by Coll's creative inhabitants since then:

> 'In the 1950s and '60s tulips and daffodils were exported from the island…the '70s and '80s saw the rise and fall of a cosmetics and perfume factory. The steadings at Breacacha Castle were once used to produce Coll's famous cheese, an industry that began in the 1850s and lasted nearly 100 years.'
>
> DISCOVER COLL LEAFLET

Sorisdale – Coll

This creative and enterprising spirit has been much in evidence throughout the **Wild Flowers of Coll and Tiree** project. A small army of islanders from both Coll and Tiree was mobilised to take photographs, write and proof-read descriptions and collate information and Emma proudly points out that the only thing that had to be done off-island was the printing. Looking through the handsome volume that she hands to me, it is evident that while the product may be island-grown, there is nothing amateurish or homespun about the results!

Inside the house I get to see the other half of this Coll based project; really a separate initiative, but wrapped together with the flower book for administrative convenience. The annually produced **Coll Magazine** has been an island institution since 1983; all articles are contributed by islanders, relatives, visitors and friends. Now Pete Mackay and Tony Oliver have developed a website with a searchable archive of all the magazines that have been published to date. At Pete's computer I select the first issue and scan the contents page: *'The Schools of Coll – 'golden rule' days of the past and present', 'COLLoquies on various island activities', 'COLL-undrums'*… a clear local focus!

At the bottom of the page I notice *'Art Collaborator : Mairi Hedderwick'*. This is the author, of 'Katie Morag' fame, who set her beautifully illustrated children's books on Struay, a fictional island reflecting Mairi's long standing relationship with Coll. Throughout the pages of the magazine, Mairi's illustrations enliven the text: a child drying off by the fire after her only set of clothes got soaked on the way home from school; a picture of a class on their knees on the beach learning to form letters in the sand; and a delightful illustration of one islander's recollection:

> **'One day we caught a lot of little crabs and let them run all over the schoolroom floor. We got the strap for that.'**
>
> COLL MAGAZINE 1983
> (*www.collmagazine.co.uk*)

Topics of interest don't change much over the years and when I rejoin the committee of the Coll Community Learning Forum in the garden, they have moved on to discuss the new wildlife learning packages, which have just been delivered to the local school. Produced by RSPB Scotland through their Nàdair **Wildlife for All** project, which followed on from the very successful **Schools Heritage** project, these provide local schools with a guide to the wildlife of their island, including species lists, a site guide and the background to special issues. There is also a starter pack of identification guides at pupil and teacher level and viewing equipment to support their activities. Recognising that it is not possible to be an expert in all things, RSPB has also made an arrangement to allow groups to spend time with wildlife specialists on their islands. I foresee crabs in the classroom again!

After a final cup of tea at Emma's, I go for a quick ramble across the machair at Totronald Reserve just up the road, where during his tenure as RSPB warden, Simon Wellock oversaw the installation of nearly 2km of fencing, along with other land management activities to

'It wasn't always plain sailing … but eventually everything pulled together.'

SIMON WELLOCK

enhance the habitat for corncrakes and breeding waders. Like many of these islands, Coll is an important bastion for the corncrake; the **Discover Coll** leaflet provides some background to this elusive bird's story:

> *'The corncrake comes from Africa and is the UK's most threatened bird. Extinct in England due to modern farming methods, this shy cousin of the coot finds a haven on Coll. Listen for its distinctive call, which has earned it nine names in Gaelic, including cleabhar-caoch, meaning "nutty noisemaker".'*

DISCOVER COLL LEAFLET

Like children, birds have a pretty good time of it on Coll and not just in the reserve at Totronald. In conjunction with the RSPB, the Coll Preservation & Wildlife Management Group has been carrying out a project to monitor the effects of predation on ground-nesting birds across the island. These birds, made particularly vulnerable by their nesting habits, lose many of their eggs and young each year to a variety of predators; the principal culprit on Coll being the ferret, a non native species which was introduced some years ago. During the project period there was a naturally occurring drop in the number of ferrets on the island, perhaps caused in turn by a myxomatosis outbreak in their primary quarry, the rabbit. Plans to trap ferrets became less practical and indeed less necessary as predation levels dropped. This may have changed the direction of the project a little, but there will be longer term benefits from the increased understanding of the dynamics of habitat and species that have developed during the process. Briefly, I ponder the Butterfly Effect theory, which proposes that the tiny change made by the beating of a butterfly's wing might trigger a whole series of interlinked events; then I make a sharp turn into project leader Rob Wainwright's track, before I start imagining one sick rabbit causing the downfall of western civilisation.

Rob, a former Scotland rugby captain, is bending from his impressive height to zip up a small person's jacket when I call in at the farmhouse. We discuss the results of the project as other Wainwright offspring come and go and then move on to an equally interesting topic; the new whale bone arch down by the pier. In 2004 the island hit the news when a 56ft fin whale was washed ashore. The National Museums of Scotland came to take the skeleton of the giant cetacean to Edinburgh, but discovered that some islanders, who resented having 'their' whale removed from the island, had detached and hidden its huge jawbone. Although the culprits were never formally identified, the bones were eventually found on a tip-off, and shipped away to Edinburgh; leaving Coll to mourn the lack of a suitable keepsake. But no longer! As I saw when I arrived on the island, there is now an authentic-looking cast of the giant mandible standing like a triumphal arch above Tammara Hedderwick's pottery at the pier, proudly proclaiming Coll as the sort of island where anything might, and often does, happen … .

Isle of Tiree

PROJECTS

'Tiree – the land below the waves ... a vivid frontier of land, sea and sky.'

TIREE – A WILDLIFE AND HERITAGE GUIDE, TIREE BUSINESS CENTRE

M.V. Clansman is churning past the short stretch of water between Coll and Tiree; a channel which marks a change in landscape and character more profound than might be expected for such a small separation. The bony backbone of Coll gives way to great dunes, but across the water on Tiree a shelving beach edges a distinctly horizontal landscape, a broad, fertile lick of greyish green, punctured by low rocks and the chalky speckles of island houses.

I am sitting over a mug of CalMac tea with the Rev. Robert Higham, who is on his way to his former parish for a stint as locum minister. Bob is an impressive figure, his height and silvery hair lend an air of gravitas, but it is his slow, resonant voice and air of perfect calm that are most striking. A career which led him from international commerce into the Church of Scotland has given him a powerful gift of persuasion, which he used to full effect to bring crofters and farmers along with him in a project to establish the 30 mile ***Tiree Pilgrimage Route' / 'Slighe Eilthireachd Thiridhe*** around the island. With an inspired piece of bargaining he even saved the ruined mediaeval ***Kilkenneth / Cill Choinnich Chapel*** from damage caused by sheltering cattle, by providing the herd with an alternative (and superior!) shed.

Led by the Tiree Heritage Society / Co Chomann Dualchas Thiriodh, the Pilgrimage Route project aimed to preserve and interpret the early Christian heritage of the island and make it accessible to people of all ages and abilities. The route more or less circumnavigates the island, visiting places that have been sacred to its inhabitants, whether the Celtic Christians, their broch-building predecessors, or churchgoers of more recent times. The guidebook, written by Bob, is available in both Gaelic and English and encompasses several levels of detail, colour coded for easy reference whilst on the move.

I have already visited the newly stabilised ruins of the chapels at ***Kirkapol*** and I have searched until I found the tiny cross inscribed stone at ***Teampall Phàraig*** on the headland of Ceann a' Bharra; but this time my goal is the Ringing Stone on the west coast near Balephetrish. Bob tells me that it emits a metallic ring when struck and that it bears a number of cup marks, surely evidence that this mysterious chime has been echoing across the shore for more than two thousand years.

> '... the Ringing Stone is a granite boulder, probably deposited by a glacier during the last Ice Age having been transported from what is now the Isle of Rhum. Clach a' Choire or Rock of the Hollow is the Gaelic name for the Ringing Stone ... according to Tiree folklore, if the stone were to be moved or shattered, the island would sink into the sea and be lost forever.'

TIREE PILGRIMAGE ROUTE – A PROJECT OF THE TIREE HERITAGE SOCIETY

With much grinding and clanking the *Clansman* berths, greatly to my relief. The landing can be hit or miss in bad weather; on a previous occasion I went all the way to Barra and back with fellow Nàdair staff member Donna Ferguson – a round trip of fourteen hours – because it looked likely that if we got off the boat at Tiree, it would be some time, maybe days, before it could come back for us!

Today, though, the prospect of a long stay on this lovely island holds no anxieties. Even at the concrete ferry-pier, the sea is a million carat jumble of azure and indigo, turquoise and viridian; its blinding points of light making rainbows between my sea-salty lashes.

Equipped with a hire car from MacLennan's garage at the end of the pier, I am soon on the way to my first island visit, to Colin Woodcock, an artist and community activist who, with his wife Susan, has made all of Tiree's exquisite spectrum the trademark of the Blue Beyond Gallery.

'We feel we have benefited as much as we have been able to give.'

COLIN WOODCOCK

Today we are discussing the layout and artwork for this book that you are now reading. Colin looks at me earnestly through blue rimmed spectacles, round and thick-glassed like portholes onto the sea. This is the last of a series of Nàdair publication projects that he has been involved in, projects which have demonstrated his passion for the island's landscape and for portraying a real sense of the place and its possibilities to visitors.

Leaving the gallery (and since this is a dream journey I can have one of Colin's raku pots and a sea-textile from Susan packed in the car to go home with me), I double back along the road from Balemartine then skirt the northern slopes of Ben Hynish, promising myself to climb up some day for a closer look at the radar station, which perches on the summit like a celestial golf ball. The road peters out in the machair above the broad expanse of Balephuil Bay and I peer out to sea looking for the thin needle of the Skerryvore Lighthouse, humming a tune by the Tiree bred band of the same name. Andy, the film-maker for the DVD that accompanies this book, bumped into the band at a ceilidh, with the result that the film has an outstanding and highly appropriate soundtrack.

Inland from the beach lies **Loch a' Phuill,** site of the **Water and Birds** project led by Tiree Rural Development, a crofter-powered force for sustainable development on the island, of which more will be said later. The loch is an internationally important Special Protection Area for waders and wildfowl, providing vital breeding and wintering grounds; it is also a vital recharge facility for the groundwater that feeds the island's taps. Drought might not be an obvious problem on the west coast of Scotland, but the manifold increase in summer population has made water deliveries from the mainland necessary in some years.

The project carried out a hydrological study of the Loch and it is now hoped that a way can be found of managing the water body to maintain summer water levels – helping both to safeguard the aquifer and to improve habitat for birds at the loch margins – while maintaining the quality and extent of the surrounding grazing lands.

I settle myself near the water's edge with my copy of **Birds of Tiree and Coll** to watch and wait, thinking of another day at another Tiree loch, two or three miles north of here. Like Loch a' Phuill, Loch Bhasapol is shallow and sandy bottomed. It too provides important bird habitat, but it was a different form of flight that I was watching that day, as my daughter Zoë skimmed jerkily across the water, learning to windsurf with local expert Willie Angus MacLean. The Nàdair project at **Loch Bhasapol** was led by the Tiree Working Group and aimed to

Brock – Isle of Tiree

'Ducks that weren't breeding here before have now come in.'

JOHN BOWLER

establish zoning and access facilities so that boarders, birds and their respective watchers could co-exist harmoniously. An unchained pair of binoculars sits at the ready in the hide, to help the casual visitor spot common or rarer species, which are written up in handy hide notes by the island's Royal Society for the Protection of Birds (RSPB) Conservation Officer, John Bowler. He missed the maiden flight of my particular fledgling though!

John and his partner Janet Hunter, a freelance ecologist, live down a sump-gutting track somewhere between the two lochs, a home that over the past few years has incubated and hatched another Nàdair project, the superbly user friendly **Birds of Tiree and Coll** book. This valuable publication charts the changing fortunes over the years of the wide range of breeding and wintering species that occur on the islands. It gives clear species accounts of all 271 species recorded, their Gaelic names and suggestions for where to go to see them. Notes on bird-related island folklore are also given, some culled from the memory of windsurfing Willie's grandfather William MacLean of Balinoe.

> *Fìor chomharra na sìde, eòin na mara a' tighinn air tìr/ A true sign of bad weather is seabirds coming ashore*
>
> 'BIRDS OF TIREE AND COLL', JOHN BOWLER AND JANET HUNTER

Today I find John Bowler out on the **Reef Reserve**, a millefiori riot in the middle of the island, lapping up against the airport's runways. The Nàdair project work on the reserve has helped to enhance this prime habitat for breeding waders, like the expostulating Lapwings (Curracag) that fly indignantly above our heads. Education is an important part of John's role with the RSPB and on guided walks visitors can enjoy seeing the pearly purple splendour of the Lapwings' feathers, while learning to avoid scaring the adults off their nests, which will leave the eggs vulnerable to the omnipresent Great Black Backed Gull (Farspag).

From the Reef it is a short step to the Rural Centre, housed in a brand new mart building next to the airport. Crofters on Tiree are acutely conscious that it is their way of life and working practices that provide the stable framework in which the island's people, economy and wildlife thrive. The relationship between crofting and wildlife is described in the **Tiree Wildlife and Heritage Guide** produced by Tiree Business Centre:

> *'It is thanks to the continuation of traditional crofting practices that wildlife, particularly bird life is so abundant. While species such as skylark, twite and starling are in decline on the mainland, Tiree is a haven for healthy densities of these birds. The success of the noisy corncrake is especially important. Once under threat of extinction in Britain, Tiree's corncrake population is now the largest in the UK, thanks to the sympathetic management of the island's rich grass meadows.'*

> *'Over the centuries, traditional use of seaweed as fertiliser on soils already enriched by blown shell sand, and grazing by livestock have created the distinctive machair habitat that is unique to the Hebrides. Between spring and autumn there is*

a spectacular succession of flowering plants, from the mauve of wild orchids in May and June, through the yellow haze of buttercups and daisies, and the reds and pinks of clover and ragged robin, to the purple knapweed in August'

Inside the Rural Centre, large displays give detailed information on the crofting way of life, while an array of farming toys keeps visiting children happy. Today there is no auction in the ring, but Jane Isaacson – one of the key figures in setting up the *Tiree Rural Development Project (TRDP)* – is helping project coordinator Ian McKinnon set up a projector for a show of pictures from the recent crofters' study tour to the Shetlands. TRDP has encompassed all sorts of activities and events, from sheep shearing workshops to farmers' markets, fundraising dances to bale wrap recycling. Jane reminds me about one of the early markets when a rather alarmed tourist was presented with a claw brandishing lobster straight off the boat – who needs packaging!

I go inside to see Flora in the office. Flora is in her twenties and soberly passionate about her crofting heritage. She wants to stay on the island and make her living here and, although she has a realistic view of the constraints facing agriculture, she has a stubborn will to do all she can to keep crofting alive and well on Tiree. Her own vivid photographic portraits of the island's landscape and livestock, sold as postcards in the Centre, are a demonstration of the creativity and adaptability of island folk.

Lachie MacFadyen is the unassuming, but very active Chair of the Centre and has spent his life as a crofter. The first time I went to see him, I was directed across a field of sheep to a distant, fast-moving figure. When I finally caught up, I was taken on a short tour of the island, before arriving in the kitchen of the MacFadyen croft where I was introduced to Lachie's wife.

Despite her husband's modesty, Mrs MacFadyen is keenly aware of the publicity value of his fundraising exploits, such as his epic row around the island – no common feat in the face of 30 miles of Atlantic swell. She had written an article about it for a magazine and it seems very appropriate that this small kitchen, with its 1950's décor and 20th century internet connection, should be broadcasting a message about sustainability, tradition and the value of vibrant island communities to the rest of the world.

I cross the Reef again to Scarinish – identifiable as the island's main village by a slightly closer gathering of houses and the presence of the bank, the police station and the Co-op. Scarinish is also where the tardis-like **An Iodhlann** is found. Pronounced 'an-ee-lun', the name of this little red 'wriggly tin' building is Gaelic for the stackyard, where the harvest is stored. In this case the crop is records of Tiree's history – letters, emigrant lists, maps, reports, photographs, stories and songs covering every aspect of life on the island and amongst its diaspora around the world.

Dr. John Holliday, Chair of Co-Roinn Ghàidhlig Thiriodh 's Cholla, which created the archive, can be hard to get hold of between surgeries and home visits, but when we meet,

'A lot of island people have become aware of our Christian heritage.'

LACHIE MACFADYEN

'We feel that we are collecting a harvest of people's memories.'

JOHN HOLLIDAY

I know I will have the undivided attention of this considerate, scholarly man. Like many of the islanders, John is a fluent Gaelic speaker and, also an island characteristic, a softly-spoken man. What is surprising, though, is that Gaelic is not his native tongue. Originally from England, Doc Holliday, as he is inevitably known, has always had an interest in the language and culture of remote places. Before coming to take up the post of GP on Tiree, he spent a number of years looking after aboriginal people at an isolated practice in Australia.

John, a team of volunteers and An Iodhlann's meticulous archivist Catriona Hunter, have turned this former reading room into a miracle of order and a gold mine of information. New enquiries and material come in every day from all over the world and the historical centre's website *www.aniodhlann.org.uk* gives virtual visitors the opportunity to access carefully chosen 'crown jewels ' from the collection, including many photographs with detailed captions, soundclips from interviews and transcripts of historic documents.

I am particularly intrigued by Tiree's traditional thatched houses or 'taighean-tughaidh', which still dominate the built landscape of the island, although many have been lost. On the website I find a photograph of a smiling, capable-looking woman, apparently taking the air on a roof garden! This turns out to be Kate MacDonald standing on the 'tobhta' of her house in Balephuil in the 1940s.

> *'Tiree's thatched houses are built with double walls, between five feet thick and six or seven feet high, filled with sand and rubble known as the hearting. Since the roof rests on the inner wall, the top of the hearting and outer wall form a wide ledge known as 'an tobhta'.*
>
> *When the walls are un-mortared this can be left open and grass and sometimes flowers grow there. In summer the dogs would often lie there in the sun and sometimes sheep would climb up to graze.*
>
> *Nowadays the spaces between the stones are usually filled with mortar so that the walls can no longer 'breathe' and the tobhta is sealed with concrete.'*
>
> AN IODLANN, TIREE'S HISTORICAL CENTRE WEBSITE
> *(www.aniodhlann.org.uk)*

In the background I can hear local genealogy expert Duncan Grant talking to a visitor: 'Well now he would have been a MacKinnon, from Kilmoluaig, but what part of the island did you say your mother's mother came from?' A couple of hours later when I leave, Duncan and the visitor are still scrolling through microfiche records, discovering new complexities to the web of family connections.

My last visit of the day brings me back to the Pilgrimage Route project and to the two chapels at **Kirkapol**. In the fading light I trace names on gravestones and then walk back across the field on the specially constructed all-abilities path.

Fiona MacKinnon, whose inspiration and hard work ensured that everyone could manage a small part of the pilgrimage, lives within sight of the chapels in the home that she first came to as a foster child from Glasgow. Many other children came and went, but Fiona stayed and became part of the family and the island community. She shows me the household copy of one of the 'Saturday Book' series, which she was given as a child to read on Sundays in lieu of more active forms of play.

This is not a relic from a previous generation – Fiona is still a young woman – but an indication of the strength of tradition that has survived on Tiree. Island culture has changed and adapted and nowadays the children are more likely to be hooked up to the community-run broadband on a Sunday than reading an improving book. But maybe both are windows on the world for a community that seems to have found a way of keeping its past alive, while embracing the challenge of living a modern life on this vivid frontier.

Colonsay & Oronsay

PROJECTS

Colonsay and Oronsay: a Wildlife and Heritage Guide

Rhododendron Clearance Initiative

Improving Access to Sites of Archaeological Interest

Celtic Priory

Oronsay Reserve (2 projects)

Corncrake & Chough Recovery (inter-island, 2 projects)

'You can choose from amongst a dozen beaches .... At Balnahard the sea is cold and you must either walk or get there by boat, but the beach is flawless, and in the little coves there are cowrie shells by the hundred.'

'COLONSAY AND ORONSAY: A WILDLIFE AND HERITAGE GUIDE' – COLONSAY COMMUNITY DEVELOPMENT COMPANY

Propping my bicycle against a rock, I step out onto the Strand, the wide stretch of sand that connects the Isles of Colonsay and Oronsay at low tide. It is a pearl-bright morning and it is scarcely possible to distinguish between the luminous grey of the cloudy sky and the slick, watery grey of the sand beneath it.

It is about a mile's walk across the Strand and these shades of grey are fitting for what is, for me, something of a walk of remembrance. John McGhie was the RSPB Area Manager for the south Argyll Islands, based on the Isle of Islay. On 18th March 2005 he made one of his regular visits to the reserve on Oronsay, opting to paddle over by kayak. Tragically, by the time he arrived on the far shore he was suffering chest pains and died at Priory Cottage on the island shortly afterwards.

I first met John on Islay, sitting in the sunshine outside his office on the Loch Gruinart Reserve on Islay. He gave the impression that relaxing in shirt sleeves with a mug of tea in one hand and a dog under his chair was a regular part of the working day – I don't know if it was – but he was certainly a man that took time have the craic with others and put them at their ease. John lent his good humoured and invaluable assistance to a variety of Nàdair projects and in the space of a couple of years I grew very fond of him. It was a great shock to hear of his untimely death at the age of 47. I nod to the choughs wheeling above Beinn Oronsay; their cries are a better valediction than I can compose and then grin as I remember the words of John's friend Robert MacNeil in his weekly column in The Scotsman: *'For many reasons, I really wish he'd lived, mainly so I could have said: "Well, where did you row from, ya daft get? Portsmouth?"'*

Keith-the-Post is just leaving as I reach the far end of the strand, the van's tyres making long silver arcs in the sand. On the shore Mike Peacock, **Oronsay Reserve** warden, is waiting for me with his Landrover. Wedged in alongside various parcels, we bump up the track between rocky hillocks, heading for the low expanse of farmland which makes up the southern half of the island, before it tails off into a shoal of rocky islets. This has to be one of my favourite places in the Hebrides – a flower studded sweep of land, fringed by pockets of the finest sand and embroidered with drystane dykes like silver cords. The Nàdair project has enabled the Reserve to bring in a stone dyker each summer for several years to rebuild the broken down sections and widen gates to allow the passage of modern farm equipment.

Mike has been fulminating through his vigorous beard for some minutes about the strictures of bureaucracy, but as we veer across the field to stop by a group of contented-looking Luing cattle, his irritation evaporates. The whole of the island of Oronsay is designated a Site of Special Scientific Interest (SSSI) and, along with a large part of southern Colonsay, a Special Protection Area (SPA) for its chough and corncrake populations. Mike manages it with a mixed farming regime, with cattle and sheep, late cut grass and arable crops. This provides suitable habitats for corncrakes, which need lots of cover for raising their young, and choughs which feed on the invertebrates found in the dung of grazing animals. Numbers of both of these rare and special species have been increasing steadily in this tailor-made environment.

'We were able to purchase a new tractor.'
MIKE PEACOCK

As we continue our tour we see lapwings and redshanks and the tiny dots of airborne skylarks, surely too high up for the decibels we are being showered with! From the crags of the island's diminutive mountain, Beinn Oronsay (93m), come the unmistakable metallic twangs of choughs calling while they indulge in impressive aerobatics – too far away to make out their smart livery of shiny black feathers with red beaks and stockings.

The sun emerges as we pass the walled fields, catching the yellow flag iris flowering in the 'corncrake corridors' – broad bands of tall herbage which provide the early season cover that the nesting birds depend on. Cover is important until the young corncrakes are fledged and independent and the fields are cut as late as possible, starting from the middle and working outwards to allow the birds to scurry away safely. Another Nàdair project, also led by RSPB, is the **Chough and Corncrake Recovery** programme, which has been encouraging farmers on Colonsay and Islay to adopt similar practices through conservation management agreements.

At the house, Val Peacock tells me about corncrake recording trips at night, when the males tune up their famous rattling cries. This is the best way of estimating numbers, as the birds are highly elusive and rarely seen – but they certainly are heard, as many sleepless islanders will tell you! Val is clear eyed, pink cheeked and a marvelous advertisement for the benefits of island dwelling. She and Mike live an isolated life, their contact with the outside word governed by the movement of tides; but they have frequent visitors and volunteers who stay for a week or two, or even longer, are accommodated in one of the prettiest cottages I know.

Just now, the island's population has doubled, with the addition of a team of stonemasons working on the island's 14th century Augustinian Priory as part of the **Celtic Priory** project. Built by the Lords of the Isles on a site which probably had supported a church since the earliest days of Celtic Christianity, the Priory is one of the most remarkable and best-preserved pre-Reformation churches in Scotland. Over the last century there have been several attempts to preserve the fabric of the buildings and the exquisite carved stones and crosses. When these earlier works were undertaken, limited knowledge of conservation techniques was available and some of the work actually accelerated the rate of deterioration.

Taking leave of Val and Mike, I make my way into the Priory enclosure. The sun is fully out now, silhouetting the smaller of the two ancient carved crosses against the sky, with choughs wheeling above it like a merry halo. Familiar figures are perched on the scaffolding; the same team that worked on Moy Castle on Mull are here and I see Duncan, the conservation contractor, in conversation with architect Martin Hadlington and Ann MacSween from Historic Scotland. The topic is 'soft topping' – not a component of a fancy dessert as I hopefully imagine, but the method by which roofless walls are capped with living turf, as a breathable form of protection against the elements – organic gortex then, rather than chocolate sauce. Apparently it works far better than the clumsy concrete capping put on the gable walls some decades ago, but the turf can be difficult to establish in the salt-laden winds. A trial area from last year is, however, doing well – scabious and knapweed are waving amongst silvery grasses above our heads.

Kiloran Bay – Colonsay

'The best thing it seems to me about Nàdair is bringing together all these islands which have been separated for the last century or so by the difficulties of travel.'

GEORGINA HOBHOUSE

The journey back across the Strand is somewhat quicker than my arrival this morning. Mike scoots me over in the Landrover before the tide gets too high. I'll no doubt see the stonemasons in the hotel bar later on, there are a few precious hours of drinking time between evening tides and they are eager for a change of scene.

Back on my bike, I head around the Atlantic coast of Colonsay, past the golf course, which is barely distinguishable from the machair and the airstrip, which used to be equally well camouflaged before its recent upgrade to accommodate scheduled flights. Soon pupils attending the High School in Oban will be able to come home at the weekend, instead of having to spend a term at a time living in the school hostel.

In a grassy hollow facing out to sea, I dismount to visit Colonsay Bookshop, a treasure trove of local interest and other books, including a fascinating antiquarian section. The shop is manned by one of Nàdair's longest standing directors, Georgina Hobhouse; witty, feisty and occasionally formidable, Georgina is well read, well travelled and keeps up a spirited battle with multiple sclerosis, which restricts her physical freedom, but most certainly not her mind. From the office, she directs me along the shelves in the shop next door to look at books she correctly surmises will be of interest to me, or to my children; when I leave I have a lavishly illustrated book of Extinct Birds, a guide to Scottish children's literature and one of the excellent and idiosyncratic little guides to these parts of the world from the 'West Highland Series' published by the Colonsay-based House of Lochar.

I rang Georgina when we first started thinking about a 'Nàdair' publication and she was, as always, full of helpful comments, information and ideas. I hope that she extracts some enjoyment from the final result and graciously overlooks its many faults!

Back on the bike, with a heavier rucksack, I continue clockwise around the island to Colonsay House; after such a hard day's work I feel I deserve tea and cakes on the lawn. Alex the Laird isn't at home just now, but if he is sensible he'll be back soon to enjoy the lovely billows of rhododendrons that line the walks and boundaries of his garden. These are the tame, friendly face of the genus Rhododendron – infinitely varied with their frilled bosses of trumpets and their leaves, large and small, some felted orange underneath, others embossed with deep branching veins. On the other sort of rhododendron, the wily and aggressive *Rhododendron ponticum*, the Laird and the islanders have declared war…with a little help from Nàdair and others.

Beyond the garden walls I follow the sound of chainsaws and a column of smoke to find the **Rhododendron Clearance Initiative** workers, Sid and Jim and Chris Nisbet from Colonsay Community Development Company which is leading the project. Chris has the unenviable task of mediating between the demands of real life and the tyranny of cashflows and grant claims to make an ambitious range of island projects happen, while Jim and Sid out here face the equally thankless task of attempting to eradicate a rampant foe, which is suppressing all other plants in its bid to take overtake the island. I am sure it is highly satisfying to see the great 30' stems of the older plants fall to the chainsaw and to burn the brash on smoking funeral pyres, but there must be nothing more depressing than looking behind you and seeing the cut stumps spring to life with barely a pause, as well as new seedlings popping up in abundance. These will be dealt with herbicide applications at a later date, dispensed from a tank on Sid's beloved 'Argocat' – an all terrain vehicle which the project paid for.

Andrew Abrahams, supplier of oysters and honey and member of the Development Company committee, appears to explain that this is a long-term project which will far outlast the Nàdair programme. Because of the obliterating effect that this deceptively handsome bush has on the island's biodiversity, a range of agencies are being persuaded to support the work in the longer term, with an eventual goal of a 'rhoddy-free' island and some useful training and employment for local people along the way.

Going back to the Community Development Co. offices, Chris puts my bike in the back of his pick-up. On the way he updates me on what's going on at Colonsay Brewery, which he runs with three other beer enthusiasts. I look up the website on the computer in Chris's office and find an apt description of him, which saves me the bother of making one up and nicely sums up the multifaceted, multitalented lives that all islanders seem to lead!

SID BOWMAN

'If Colonsay's future is tourism we need to get rid of rhododendrons.'

ANDREW ABRAHAMS

> *'Chris Nisbet is Colonsay's Island Development Officer but as nothing much has happened here for the last 25 years we often wonder what he does. When he's not developing the island or brewing he runs his croft and is still finishing off building his own home. Chris is also the assistant electricity supply engineer and a fireman. The electricity job works well with brewing because when the power goes off, the brewery grinds to a halt and Chris is free to go and fix the fault. Chris also works on the pier at ferry times and seems to spend a lot of time attending mainland conferences of strange organisations, but at least he can bring some ingredients back with him.'*
> (www.colonsaybrewery.co.uk)

Returning to more serious matters (although I *am* looking forward to a pint in the Hotel later) I get my first look at *'Some Archaeological Sites on Colonsay'*, a handsome leaflet produced by the Development Company and written by Kevin Byrne, long time Colonsay resident and island history expert – as well as harbour master, author, publisher, holiday accommodation provider, tour guide, skipper and one-time hotelier.

Every step on this island is a foot planted in the past and I am fascinated to discover that the carved stone with the face of a man I saw earlier in the day in the grounds of Colonsay House was once a well cover in the now-abandoned village of Riasg Buidhe on the east side of the island:

> *'The stone is known locally as 'Dealbh na Leisge' which translates as the 'image of sloth' or the 'sleepy figure'. In point of fact, the face is that of a bearded cleric, with the distinctive tonsure of the northern church, and wearing robes that fall in such a way as to create the early Christian symbol of a fish .... Viewed from the other*

side, one can recognise a portent fertility symbol, suggesting that the 9th century Viking inhabitants of Colonsay sought to incorporate some aspects of traditional beliefs within their Christianity'

'SOME ARCHAEOLOGICAL SITES IN COLONSAY' – COLONSAY COMMUNITY DEVELOPMENT COMPANY

The leaflet, which was edited by Georgina Hobhouse, lists seven of the most interesting and accessible sites out of Colonsay's wealth of archaeology. Chris tells me that islander Bill Lawson is making marker posts, which will soon be put in place to help walkers to find the sites and that bracken is being controlled to ensure that the archaeology remains visible during the summer months; good news for those, like me, who have forced their way hopelessly through armies of ticks and towering fronds trying to find an ancient chapel or a mediaeval field system!

There is time for one last bicycle ride before the evening ferry which will take me on to Islay and I head up to the north west of the island to the spectacular Kiloran Bay. The RSPB Landrover is parked up the hill, Mike is taking advantage of suitable tides to check up on the Colonsay choughs. Two figures are heading north towards Balanahard, Ann from Historic Scotland and Martin the architect; I join them and we head off to look for Sguid nam Ban Truagh, or Shelter of the Miserable Women, which sounds like an intriguing, if not very cheerful, goal. We don't quite make it and have to turn back under the tyranny of the relentlessly on-time CalMac scheduling, but not before locating the remains of the chapel and nunnery of Cill Chatriona. Here also is Clach na Pheanis, or the Stone of Penance. Women clearly did not have a terribly jolly time in this corner of the island!

Bicycle flung into the back of the car, we only just make it in time to be herded onto the ferry by Kevin Byrne, nautically bearded and looking every inch the efficient piermaster that he is (amongst everything else!). I cast a regretful glance up the hill to the trim white hotel and the red telephone box outside (which is used to nurture germinating vegetable seeds rather than long distance relationships) and think about that foaming pint that I never had … something to look forward to next time.

'Some of the things we have here are absolutely outstanding … we are very happy to share them with everybody that we can'.

KEVIN BYRNE

Jura

PROJECTS

Jura Heritage, Access and Interpretation

Butterflies & Burnet Moths: A Recovery Programme (inter-island)

Heritage Tourism Training (inter-island)

'The name Jura is probably from the Norse Dýr ey, Island of Deer.'

'WELCOME TO JURA – ISLAND OF DEER', JURA DEVELOPMENT TRUST

The first leg of the journey to Jura takes me to tiny Port Askaig on Islay. There is not much here – a hotel, the berth for the Jura ferry and a rather smart new road snaking up the cliff – but there is always something going on. This evening, the small port is overwhelmed with tall, hearty looking Dutchmen, arrived back from a visit to Jura's solitary, but rather excellent distillery.

I plan to spend the night over on Jura and catch up with a few folk in the evening, before starting my round of visits on Islay tomorrow, so I execute a quick turnaround to catch the little ferry over the Sound and into the shadow of the glittering cones of the Paps of Jura. A copy of the Jura Development Trust's **'Welcome to Jura'** leaflet helps me identify them – nearest is Beinn a' Chaolais, 'Peak of the Sound'; then Beinn an Òir, 'Mountain of Gold'; and a little to the east Beinn Shiantaidh, 'Peak of the Storms'.

Jura is the third largest of the Argyll Islands after Mull and Islay, but its residents are fond of quoting the revealing statistic that the deer population outnumbers the human population by approximately 30:1! A glance at the topography is sufficient to understand why; the landscape is rugged, rising from the uninhabited west coast into high and lonely moors before descending to the more hospitable eastern shores, where startling evidence of a milder climate can be seen in the cordylines flourishing in the hotel's garden and in the magnificent organic walled gardens at Jura House.

This evening I am travelling only a few miles up the island's only road, to reach Craighouse, the only settlement of any size. The sky is tinged pink and orange, without a breath of wind. It couldn't be less like one autumn day when I arrived here with a group of Nàdair folk on a 'Grand Tour' of each other's projects, organised as part of the **Heritage Tourism Training** project by Highlands and Islands Enterprise.

We had come by charter boat on from the mainland. The voyage on *Sea Leopard* and *Gemini* had seemed like an appealing prospect, until we came out of the sheltered inland waters at the Dorus Mòr, a subdued cousin of the famous Corrievreckan Whirlpool at the north end of Jura. Suddenly we were in huge waves, which left us suspended briefly in mid air on the downward slope, only to crash jarringly onto our seats as the boat heaved back onto the next crest.

On *Gemini* with one half of the party, I felt confident that we would at least make it – having previously survived several 'exciting' trips with captain Mike Murray. Sea Leopard had vanished, but was presumably hugging the lee of Jura's shore. Scanning the coast to see if I could spot her, I could just make out the most northerly of Jura's landing points, Kinuachdrachd pier, but not well enough to examine the work that the Jura Development Trust had carried out to stabilise it and bring it back into use. Up above on the hill, the white dot of Barnhill, the house that George Orwell lived in while he was writing '1984', was just visible through the rain.

'We wanted people to feel welcomed and happy, and to feel the value of standing in this spot at this time.'

ELAINE CAMPBELL

Finally, the waves dropped a little as we came in to land. At that moment nothing about the Jura looked hospitable, except the ever impeccably dressed and imperturbably calm Elaine Campbell, Jura Development Trust project officer, waiting to welcome us on the pier. Things did start to get better, however, as we tottered ashore to be ushered into the warm, dry Jura bus, which rocked no more than absolutely necessary over the odd pothole on the way down the road to Craighouse.

By the next morning, our party had, without exception, fallen in love with this wild and welcoming island. If some still felt the ground heaving gently beneath their feet, it probably had more to do with a reception at the Feolin Study Centre the evening before, followed by a late night in the hotel bar.

Soon all were found joyfully crowding round an interpretation board in eager discussion about materials, layout, mounting, print colour and what constitutes too much or too little information. It was a sight to gladden my heart and I took a photograph to demonstrate to my children that there are other people in the world that wouldn't think it strange to examine every interpretation board in exhaustive detail.

The board was part of the **Jura Heritage, Access and Interpretation** project to improve visitor access to and enjoyment of the island, including leaflets, signage and the upgrade of Kinuachdrachd pier – the nearest harbour to the Corrievreckan whirlpool.

For many visitors the wildlife is the key draw to Jura, but our Nàdair party, familiar with the elusive nature of island wildlife, were just a little suspicious when an otter trotted up beside our bus as we came back to Craighouse after our island tour. Elaine has the dark hair and pale skin of a Celtic enchantress, but she claimed that she had nothing to do with it, just like she had nothing to do with the spectacular rainbows that arced over almost every view we were encouraged to admire during our visit!

> *'The skies are patrolled by majestic Golden Eagles and the larger Sea Eagles, whilst out to sea, Arctic Skuas harry Common Terns and Arctic Terns heading back to their nests with a cargo of fish.*
>
> *Along the shore, look out for hunting otters and basking seals. The best time to see otters is in the early morning or evening. When all you see is a head in the water, it can be hard to tell if it's a seal or an otter. Wait until it dives – a seal will just sink, while an otter will leap forward, often showing its tail as it dives.'*
>
> 'WELCOME TO JURA – ISLAND OF DEER', JURA DEVELOPMENT TRUST

Wildlife on a smaller scale was spotted by Paul Kirkland of Butterfly Conservation Scotland, who pointed out the communal silk webs of the Marsh Fritillary butterfly and explained that counting these webs is often the most reliable method of monitoring the fortunes of this threatened species.

Marsh Fritillaries, along with Transparent and Slender Scotch Burnets, were the focus of Butterfly Conservation's Nàdair project, **Butterflies and Burnet Moths: A Recovery Programme for the Argyll Islands** which aimed to find out more about the distribution and needs of these species, as well as promoting their conservation. A series of workshops led by project officer Tom Prescott trained island volunteers and information leaflets were provided to farmers in key areas. The Marsh Fritillary leaflet explains just how important land management practices are to the survival of this threatened species:

> *'The long-term survival of the Marsh Fritillary, as with many other species, requires a patchwork of linked sites enabling an exchange of adults between neighbouring colonies …. A degree of light grazing, preferably by cattle, is essential to maintain flower-rich areas and devil's-bit scabious* (the caterpillar's sole food plant) *in an open sward.'*
>
> LEARN ABOUT THE MARSH FRITILLARY – BUTTERFLY CONSERVATION SCOTLAND

I am jolted back to the present from my musings on that previous island visit by the sight of the characteristic checkerboard pattern of oranges, creams, browns and blacks of an adult Marsh Fritillary flying in the last of the day's sunshine. It is pleasurable to see the butterfly's lifecycle completed in the same spot that I saw it begin and I think how lucky I have been that the Nàdair programmes have given me the opportunity to visit these amazing islands in all weathers and in all seasons.

Pulling up at the hotel, there's a rainbow over Craighouse bay and I can see Elaine already waiting for me in the bar. It occurs to me that I might just finally get that pint of island ale that I missed on Colonsay.

Islay

PROJECTS

Discover Islay & Jura Leaflet

Woollen Mill Renovation & Workshop

Islay Community Access (2 projects)

Finlaggan Development & Environmental Improvements

Nerabus Burial Ground and Carved Stones

Finlaggan Interpretation Hub

Loch Gruinart Reserve Land & Countryside Management
(2 projects)

Smaull Farm Land & Countryside Management
(2 projects)

Mull of Oa Land and Countryside Management

Bun Othan Harbour

Seanchas Ìle

'Nam b' eileanach mi gum b' Ìleach mi' / 'Were I an islander I should be an Islay man.'

PROVERB COLLECTED BY THE SEANCHAS ÌLE PROJECT

'When visitors come down through my land I can say with pride "Go down there, you'll enjoy going to the island."'

DONALD BELL

My visit to Islay starts at Finlaggan, the historic, if not geographic, heart of the island. The three tiny islets on Loch Finlaggan were the centre of the Lordship of the Isles, presided over between the 14th and 16th centuries by the MacDonalds, descendants of the legendary Somerled.

> *'The Lords of the Isles ruled the islands and part of the west coast of Scotland, from Kintyre to Lewis, virtually independent of royal control. The heir to a strong Gaelic and Norse tradition, the Lord of the Isles – ill Innse Gall – was one of the most powerful figures in the country with the small islands in Loch Finlaggan a centre of symbolic and administrative importance.'*
>
> FINLAGGAN TRUST WEBSITE
> *(www.finlaggan.com)*

Here at Finlaggan the Lords were installed as rulers of their flourishing realm; here they held their councils, prayed in their church and buried their dead – and here the Finlaggan Trust is now uncovering this long neglected aspect of Scotland's history; protecting its relics and firing the imagination of an ever increasing number of visitors.

The **Finlaggan Development and Environmental Improvements** project was the first Nàdair project to be carried out by the Finlaggan Trust; consolidating the mediaeval chapel on Eilean Mor/Large Island and protecting the beautiful carved graveslabs which lay within its walls. This inspired a second project to conserve other carved memorial stones, this time at **Nerabus Burial Ground**, near Port Charlotte, about 15 miles from Finlaggan. Today I am here to see the third and most ambitious project and, as I pass the rounded bulk of a standing stone above the loch, I can see that it is in full swing and nearing completion.

Donald Bell meets me at the visitor centre, a low stone cottage, which is now being joined by a new structure, turned at right angles to the original building, with a huge gable window facing the loch. I know perfectly well that Donald has cajoled, charmed and even bullied this project, the **Finlaggan Interpretation Hub**, into life against overwhelming odds of time, money and personal circumstance – but he raises his shoulders and his resplendent eyebrows in a gesture of innocent astonishment as he shows me around, as if it all just happened by itself!

There is a rumour in the Nàdair office that Donald can walk on water; and I suspect it may be true. I have seen him gallantly rescuing fellow Nàdair project leader Amber Knight, when her borrowed wellies deserted her on a visit to the Finlaggan islands; but it is Donald's success in getting a building up in record time – on an island where builders are usually too busy to quote and materials have to be shipped in by ferry – that is nothing short of miraculous.

As we step over cables and around busy electricians, I can see how this new building is going to make a huge difference to the visitor experience. For a start, the big window gives a fantastic view down to the loch and the islands – not everyone wants to negotiate the paths

and boardwalks in all weathers, even with the benefit of one of the Centre's numerous pairs of 'courtesy wellies'. There will also be more space to tell the story of Finlaggan and of the six years of archaeological excavation that have just been completed. Many of the finds are currently held at the National Museums of Scotland in Edinburgh, but with the provision of appropriate facilities, it is likely that some will come back to Islay soon.

There are some things about Finlaggan that don't appear to be changing, however. A pot of tea is brewing in the old cottage, cake tins are being opened and a bottle of Finlaggan malt is on hand, in case the tea needs a bit of extra heat. Members of the committee, Rona MacKenzie, Gina McAuslan, Hugh MacDonald, Jean MacKay and Lynda MacArthur, have all found the time to pop in to say hello. It is this sort of welcome that makes places like Finlaggan so special – it is not just a museum, but part of the daily lives and enthusiasms of real people.

Warmed by the hospitality as much as the tea, I say my goodbyes and am handed into my car by the ever-gallant Donald, before heading off up the road to my next stop, the **Islay Woollen Mill**, just a few miles up the road.

The Woollen Mill is most emphatically not a museum piece, although there has been a weaver here since 1550. Gordon Covell is the present incumbent, maintaining traditions, skills and veteran machinery in order to design and produce top quality woven fabrics. Some of Gordon's products have achieved world-wide exposure in the films 'Braveheart', 'Rob Roy' and 'Forrest Gump', as well as appearing on the catwalk in the collections of the Chanel fashion house.

Inside the mill there is nothing of the hushed couture boutique; all is noise and movement – clashing metal, whirring belt drives and oily gears and fascinating contraptions with anthropomorphic names like Slubbing Billy and Spinning Jenny. It is not, however, the internal workings that have been the subject of the mill's Nàdair project and Gordon attends to a few switches and levers before accompanying me over to the oldest building on the site, the Grade A listed Waulkmill.

Perched on the riverbank below an arched bridge, this was an empty shell until the Nàdair project led by Islay Estates and the Islay Development Company restored it for use as a training workshop for traditional handlooming. The atmosphere inside is more Thomas Hardy than Dickens – a shaft of dusty light falls on Gordon's sure hands as he deftly throws the shuttle to and fro and thumps the beater against the weft. A piece made by a student is stretched, unfinished, on another loom, glowing soft russet and loden green.

A car draws up outside and Gordon heads back over to the mill shop to cater to his customers' requirements. A flat cap to keep out the Scottish weather, perhaps? (Did you know that 2500 cloth caps can be made from one bolt of cloth?) Or maybe a woolly Braveheart scarf?

'We can raise the water levels for wildfowl in the winter ...'

JAMES HOW

I linger for a moment to watch the sun striking the river through rough green wych elm leaves. This was one of the earlier Nàdair projects and the Waulkmill already looks as if it never suffered the ignominy of ruin. I recall many phone calls with Michael MacRae of Islay Development Company, discussing the oak flooring, the new window frames and a host of other tenuously connected subjects. A native of Lewis, Michael had the most melodious voice and a gift of the gab to match it.

Which reminds me, there is no time for idling away today! Islay is a big island and there are still a lot of projects to see. I shout my goodbyes through the mill door and head off up the lane, hoping that whatever cosy gear the visitors come away with won't be needed for at least the next day or two.

At pretty Bridgend village I turn right to skirt the top of Loch Indaal, then northwards over the narrow neck of land that separates it from **Loch Gruinart**. This is one of three RSPB reserves on Islay – the others are **Smaull Farm** on the Rhinns of Islay and **The Oa,** the dramatic cliff-fringed southern corner of the island.

Approximately one third of the 1600 hectare Loch Gruinart reserve is farmed, using crops and livestock as habitat management tools to benefit wildlife – a clear demonstration that farming and wildlife can go hand in hand. The rest is made up of mud flats and salt marshes and a large area of heather moorland. The Nàdair project here, as on the other Islay reserves, encompasses a wide range of habitat enhancement measures, from hydrological management of the wetlands and blanket bog, to developing corncrake corridors along field margins and chough nesting sites in deserted buildings. Together this huge area offers a wide range of habitats and, no matter what time of the year it is, there is always something to see. Perhaps the most spectacular month is October, when around 20,000 barnacle and white-fronted geese return from Greenland for the winter

Today I am joining a guided walk led by James How, Land Operation Manager at Loch Gruinart. I am a bit late and they have already made their way from the visitor centre to the edge of the wetland area. Catching up, I can see what is unmistakably James' wild head of hair, barely controlled by a sturdy bandana, as he stands on a bench to explain the management of the low lying fields at the head of the loch.

He points out the sea wall which separates the seasonally flooded fields from the salt marshes in the bay, explaining that this area was first reclaimed from the sea by Dutch settlers. The wet fields make an ideal habitat for breeding waders, including lapwings, redshanks, curlews and snipe at this time of year and then later on for overwintering wildfowl, when large numbers of teal and wigeon can be seen, also mallard, shoveler, golden-eye and pintail ducks. A series of sluices, installed as part of the Nàdair land management project on the reserve, allows the water levels to be manipulated throughout the year to suit the needs of different species.

In mid-sentence James suddenly pauses to point out a Hen Harrier flying low over the wetland and twelve pairs of binoculars sweep round to follow his gesture. This is the pair that featured in last year's BBC 'Springwatch', and James has known them for years, observing them and monitoring their productivity. Incompetent with artificial magnification, I rely on the naked eye and follow the flinty grey and black form as it contours up towards the moorland. We are rewarded by the sight of the female bird exploding upwards from her nest in the heather to execute an agile mid air collection of the food that her partner has brought. The moor where they are nesting was drained at one time in a bid to bring it into agricultural production, but the Nàdair project has seen ditches blocked up to help restore the valuable blanket bog habitat.

Time passes quickly once we settle into the hide out in the middle of the wetland area. Nothing could be more pleasant than a sea-scented afternoon breeze coming through the open windows, the occasional subdued exclamation of enthusiasm from the company and the keen eyes of an expert to identify the teeming birdlife.

I can't help noticing that James' eyes are different colours and find myself imagining that this might be the happy effect of many hours spent scanning this patchwork of water and meadow. Clearly one afternoon isn't enough, however, because when I check my own eyes later, they are still a disappointingly uniform khaki.

Unfortunately there isn't time to go to Small Farm and see the results of habitat enhancement work for Corncrakes and Choughs, but with any luck I'll get down to the Oa reserve tomorrow. I have one more call down to the southern tip of the Rhinns of Islay to fit in today, to see the **Bun Othan Harbour** project at Port Wemyss. This was a latecomer to the Nàdair programme, made possible by a little spare funding in the coffers.

I have never had the pleasure of meeting the team that laid out the new footpath, planted its edges with wildflowers, created a picnic area and installed interpretative signage, and I'm missing out this time too, as Calum Anderson, whom I'd hoped to see, is off the island just now. But down by the shore there are seals to keep me company and I am happy just to sit and enjoy the view of the Rhinns lighthouse on the tiny Isle of Orsay and the pretty twin villages of Port Wemyss and Portnahaven. Apparently these two planned 19th century villages are quite individual communities, although they share a church and are separated only by a bridge. Mind you, the church does have two doors and I recall being told that the parishioners of Portnahaven enter strictly by one door and the parishioners of Port Wemyss by the other. Quirky to be sure, but somewhat characteristic of what I have seen of island life; where rivalries and insults are held onto from generation to generation, but rarely allowed to interfere with the rhythms of daily life, or the customs of good neighbours.

Day two on Islay sees me up bright and early and making my way to the old fever hospital on the edge of the island's main settlement, Bowmore. I'm not suffering from anything more serious than a bout of curiosity though, as the building, refurbished and extended, now houses Ionad Chaluim Chille Ìle/The Columba Centre in Islay. The Centre operates in partnership with the Gaelic College on Skye, Sabhal Mòr Ostaig, providing a range of courses in Gaelic language, and it has also been the home of the Nàdair project *Seanchas Ìle* through which some of the island's heritage and folklore has been collected and recorded in the unique Islay dialect.

Ionad Chaluim Chille Ìle is not just a college, but more of a Gaelic community centre, providing a venue for social events, music and art. I have pleasurable memories of evening sunshine and jazz, watching little threads of cirrus through the rooflights of the performance space. Dòmhnall Angaidh MacIllinnein, the irrepressible manager of the Columba Centre is here to meet me. He is engagingly modest about his own achievements and eloquently enthusiastic about those of others – including on occasion Nàdair's, I am pleased to say! By the time the Seanchas Ìle coordinator Emily Edwards joins us, I have been well briefed on all the hard work she has put into organising the project, interviewing islanders, getting the website up and running and putting together the book that will be the culmination of the project.

I join Emily in the library to listen to some of the stories she has recorded in nearly two years on Islay. She tells me that it took a little while to become accepted by the older members of the community; nothing personal, just a certain amount of astonishment that someone, and an attractive young woman at that, should want to speak with them in Gaelic!

I wish I could understand the recordings, rich expressive voices interspersed with Emily's own clear tones and, at times, much laughter, then tantalising lapses into English, whether as a necessary part of the story, or just the unconscious shift of a bilingual speaker, I cannot tell.

Listening to these lilting voices I can see how Emily might have come to a career in Gaelic through her love of traditional music. Originally from Easter Ross, an area with a much lower proportion of Gaelic speakers than Islay, she was surprised by how little traditional music was played here. She has, however, done her best to remedy this by teaching fiddle and taking part in regular traditional music sessions at the Port Charlotte Hotel.

I turn to reading the English transcripts, while the soft Gaelic voices play on in the background and give me the illusion of being present at the tellings. This 'story that Donald MacFadyen heard' appeals to me for the way it reveals the poetry in the Gaelic language, as well as its self-deprecating humour:

> '*A crofter without much English is trying to explain to the Lowland vet what happened to his cow. In Gaelic he wanted to say: "Chaidh i faotainn ann an sùil-chrith agus cha do chnàmh i a cìr fad trì làithean às a dhèidh." (She was in a deep bog and she never chewed the cud for three days.)*
> *The crofter translated the Gaelic literally which in English came out as:*
> "*She was in the eye of the earth and she never boned her comb for three whole days.*"'

SEANCHAS ÌLE – CRUINNEACHADH, CLÀRACHADH AGUS GLEIDHEADH DUALCHAS GÀIDHLIG ÌLE / SEANCHAS ÌLE – COLLECTING, RECORDING AND PRESERVING ISLAY'S GAELIC HERITAGE

I'm leaving the island by Port Ellen this afternoon, catching the ferry to Kennacraig on Kintyre, but there is still plenty of time for a walk and maybe even a swim before then. The road that leads east out of Port Ellen, skirting rocky coves and tiny beaches, is a pilgrimage route for whisky lovers. I keep going resolutely past Laphroaig then Lagavulin, where the Lord of the Isle's fleet used to anchor in the bay below Dunivaig Castle, but pull in when I see the whitewashed walls of Ardbeg distillery. I'm not yet in pursuit of a dram, however – I have been brought up to believe that such a pleasure can only be earned by a good dose of fresh air and exercise beforehand, preferably somewhere boggy, with a great deal of uphill.

The Ardbeg to Solam walk, part of the **Islay Community Access** project, more or less qualifies, although it might not meet the rigorous standards of a Munro-basher. The group just arriving back down the track look rosy and well satisfied with their efforts. This is the 'Walkaboutabit' group, launched by the Community Access project in tandem with Islay Healthy Living Centre and the Scotland-wide 'Paths to Health' initiative. Walks are led by volunteer guides, or by project officer Lindy MacLellan.

Lindy surely embodies the benefits of getting out and about in the countryside. I know it is a cliché, but it is hard not to imagine that there is energy fizzing out of her auburn curls. She doesn't appear to live up to the other bit of the redhead formula though, as nobody without endless resources of patience could have achieved what she has done in terms of negotiating agreements with farmers, organizing contractors and building a sense of ownership in the community. These paths are much appreciated by visitors, whether for informal walking or as part of the annual Islay Walking Festival, but they are also very much part of the daily lives of many islanders, perhaps because each route has been identified and selected through a local consultation process.

Around twenty routes have already been created through Phase 1 and Phase 2 of the project and there is no intention of stopping now. Phase 3, which will take the Islay Community Access project beyond the Nàdair programme, is already well into the planning stage. In some cases the routes require major works to build new paths, in other places just the addition of a kissing gate, a bridge, or a safe place to pull a car off the road has made the island's countryside more accessible.

The Walkaboutabit group heads off in search of a cup of tea, leaving me to a solitary ramble. I set off thinking it's a shame to have missed the craic, but as I start the climb up Airigh nam Bèist (place, or shelter of the beast or animals and, coincidentally, the name of one of Ardbeg's malts) I start to appreciate the benefits of a solo visit to this atmospheric place.

'Ardbeg to Solam – A scenic walk to a haunting spot on the hillside. Solam was inhabited until the 1930s, but in the late 18th century the nearby community was wiped out by the plague. When all the inhabitants were known to be dead, the buildings were burned. Outlines of some of the houses can still be traced in the glen close to the surviving ruin.'

'EXPLORE ISLAY LEAFLET, NINE GUIDED WALKS AROUND THE ISLAND OF ISLAY' – ISLAY COMMUNITY ACCESS GROUP (*www.islayaccess.org*)

A bit of a mist has come in as I hurry back down the hill, not a cold mist, but eerie nonetheless. It thickens as I drive back through Port Ellen and gathers ever closer as I head off for my last call on the island. The cliffs of the Oa, the high headland that guards the western side of Port Ellen are spectacular. From the American Monument, which commemorates the loss of HMS Tuscania in 1918, the Isle of Rathlin and the Antrim coast of Northern Ireland can be seen. In the era of the Kingdom of Dalriada and the later Lordship of the Isles, the sea was the highway in these parts and Antrim would have been a closer neighbour to Islay than most of mainland Scotland.

My reason for coming here is because the **Mull of Oa** is the RSPB's newest reserve on Islay. The Nàdair project here involved the development of infrastructure to manage and maintain suitable habitats for the wide range of birds that occupy the varied landscape of the headland.

Thanks to BBC 'Springwatch', millions of viewers across the UK know that you don't pronounce the 'a' in Oa. The same lucky people had the privilege of seeing young choughs leaving their nest and the resident golden eagles soaring above the cliffs. Today I doubt that I will have the same luck, but there is nonetheless an ethereal splendour to the place as I make my way down to the shore through the fog. The pagoda roofs of the distilleries already give Islay a faintly incongruous oriental air, but here I feel as if I am walking into a Chinese ink and wash painting. Islets in the bay heave up in monochrome craggieness and the sea laps into an invisible horizon. A solitary gull bobs on the surface and I can hear the twanging cries of invisible choughs.

Kelp slithers round my legs as I swim out from the shore, it feels like tough, pliable skin and I can imagine that I am a Selkie – human on shore, but donning my seal skin to swim back to an ocean home. Penetrating cold soon reminds me that CalMac ferries are rather more reliable than Scottish folklore, so I haul myself out of the now unpleasantly clinging, seaweed, jog up the cliff path and turn the car heater up full on the road to the pier.

Gigha

PROJECT

Achamore Gardens

Gigha is breathtaking – sandy beaches, clear green seas, a host of wildlife .... There are also world renowned Gardens to explore – viewed by the islanders as the "Jewel in the Crown".

ISLE OF GIGHA HERITAGE TRUST

MALCOLM MACNEILL

'We have managed to do a lot of restoration work. It's given us a great opportunity.'

MICKY LITTLE

Gigha is the southernmost of the Nàdair islands, not quite in the tropics, but still boasting an impressive array of exotic plants for an island off the coast of the Mull of Kintyre. It is the salt-laden wind that is the great enemy of gardeners in this maritime region, but **Achamore Gardens,** the jewel of Gigha, lie in the lee of the island's spine and are enclosed by mature woodlands which shield them from the worst of the Atlantic storms.

Of necessity, few west coast gardens benefit from the spectacular sea views that surround them, but once inside the vital shelter belt at Achamore, there is a different, balmy world of luxuriant greens, with flamboyant oranges, pinks, yellows and crimsons cascading from one of the UK's most extensive collections of rhododendrons and azaleas.

These plants were the passion of Sir James Horlick (yes, he of hot drinks fame), who from 1944 created a complex and beautiful garden of over 20 hectares. Sir James bequeathed his plant collection, but not the garden itself, to the National Trust for Scotland and, after his death in 1971, Achamore House and Gardens passed through a succession of ownerships.

In 2001 Gigha made world news with its 'community buy-out' which saw the islanders acquire the whole of the island. The purchase included Achamore Gardens, which are now managed, along with all the other community assets, by the Isle of Gigha Heritage Trust. Gigha has hardly been out of the news ever since, with the legendary Willie MacSporran at the helm, the Heritage Trust has taken on project after project – new community housing, the 'Dancing Ladies' wind turbines, a quarry, the hotel.

Today I'm meeting Malcolm McNeill, former head gardener, who began working at Achamore in 1968 and only recently retired from his post. I've asked Malcolm before what the secret of his youthfulness is; he claims that it is over three decades of drinking the water from a certain nearby spring. I'm not sure whether to believe him, but it does lead me to speculate whether, actually, he has leaped the boundary into immortality – there was a Malcolm MacNeill, Laird of Gigha in the 15th century and don't all great men turn to gardening in their later years?

Malcolm knows the gardens inside out; the name of every plant, which storm blew down each fallen tree. I once foolishly revealed that I have a degree in Horticulture, so he uses gardener's shorthand with me, never calling a plant by its full name. 'See the 'Madame le Coultre' over there,' he says, pointing to a vegetation bedecked wall. To be truthful I'm not sure if I'm admiring a Rose or a Clematis, but I try to nod knowledgeably.

When the Trust acquired the Island and the garden in 2001, Malcolm had been maintaining this huge site almost single-handed for years. I remember his catalogue of 'things that need to be done now' when I first visited the garden on a very wet, late winter day. Drainage was at the top of the list. The grounds had a network of drains, but over the years ditches had become blocked, tree roots had cracked the pipes and whole sections of the garden were suffering from waterlogging. Another urgent need was the restoration of the shelterbelt, which had suffered considerable damage in winter storms; then there was restoring the plant collection – some specimens had been lost over the years – not to mention replacing the elderly glasshouse in the walled garden.

It was an expensive wish list, but given several decades of limited investment, not an unreasonable one. The **Achamore Gardens** project was put together within the Nàdair programme to get a comprehensive programme of restoration off the ground, involving new staff, significant investment and a lot of very hard work.

There is a new Head Gardener now, Micky Little, who moved to the island with his family in October 2006. The drains are working, stone walls and greenhouses have been repaired and I can see that there has been an enormous amount of work put into renovating the old borders and creating stunning new plantings.

Malcolm McNeill had nearly forty years in Achamore Gardens. When he started, his boss, Malcolm Allen, had been head gardener for half a century! I haven't yet had the pleasure of meeting Micky; with any luck, there will be plenty of time for me to come back one of these decades and take a walk round the garden with him … but I think I'll brush up a bit on my plant identification before then!

String statue – Gigha

Luing

PROJECT
Heritage Interpretation

'Luing has exceptional natural heritage assets to be explored by the visitor ....
The annual toad migration is one of Luing's natural wonders!'

ISLE OF LUING COMMUNITY TRUST

Clachan Bridge arcs solidly over the narrow sound to the Isle of Seil, bearing up under the strain of tractors, tour buses and even the occasional highland wedding. It is a pretty spot, but today Seil is a transit point rather than a destination – I'm on my way to the Isle of Luing.

Many Luing residents would like to have a bridge, but Cuan Sound is a challenging stretch of water and for now the crossing from Seil is made only by boat. Sea kayakers are surfing in the standing waves today and the resident otter pops up for a look at the ferry. I'm still watching for him to resurface when the ramp grinds onto the slip at the far side.

Alastair Fleming meets me and we set off for the village of Cullipool. As Chair of the Isle of Luing Community Trust, Alastair has experienced all of the ups and downs of managing a complex project on a small island. He is disarmingly frank about the setbacks the community has had to face over the past few years, which resulted in a far less ambitious Nàdair project than they had first hoped for.

There appears, however, to be no sense of defeat amongst the members of the committee when we meet at the Fleming's cottage. Rightly so; they may not yet have managed to build the museum that they had planned, but, through a separate initiative, outside the Nàdair programme, the Trust has bought open land around the village, mineral rights to the disused quarries and the remains of the old quarry engine shed.

Some of this land had been intended to provide the site for the new museum, but the purchase proved hugely complicated and could not be completed in time for the building to go ahead within the Nàdair programme. Undaunted, however, the Luing folk are now viewing this as an opportunity to re-think the project, seek new funding and take it forward in a way that better fits their evolving needs.

'In the end 20% of the population was involved in one way or another.'

JULIA GALBRAITH

This isn't to say that a Nàdair supported project wasn't completed on Luing – the **Heritage Interpretation** project provided interpretative signage, walk leaflets and welcome seating to help visitors get the most out of exploring the island. Julia Galbraith was my main contact for the project and, like so many of the people I have encountered on this journey, she is modest about her own achievements, describing instead the hard work put in by Peter Hooper who managed the project, Mike Barlow who assisted him, Phil Robertson who supervised the building of the plinths and the members of Luing History Group who researched the subject matter of the panels.

We take a walk through the village to admire one of the interpretation boards, set on a pleasing plinth of local slate, which already looks as if it has been there for ever. This is an island with many interesting stories: wildlife, farming, quarrying, antiquities, landscape and geology all feature on boards around the island.

Apart from the ubiquitous and famous Luing cattle, the most noticeable characteristic of the island is the legacy of the slate mining industry. The village of Cullipool is postcard perfect now, rows of whitewashed quarriers' cottages nestle under a cliff, looking out over the bluest

of seas towards the Garvellach Islands, but it must once have been a dangerous, swarming hive of industry. Pretty, but perilously steep-sided lagoons pockmark the land around the village and perched on the edge of one is the shell of the Engine Shed, the future home of the Luing Museum. It is not hard to imagine that this still strangely unknown island will soon become a magnet for visitors.

Heading back to the ferry, I decline the offer of a lift and walk back round the shore to Cuan Sound. I want to savour the last moments of this special journey around the Argyll Islands before I cross to Seil – the island that was my home for the four years I spent with Nàdair – and head back to my new life on the Black Isle.

The sun is dipping and there is a flat, slaty light over the Firth of Lorne. The islands of Belnahua, Fladda and the Garvellachs are close inshore; beyond them lie all of the Nàdair islands, suspended on the pewter sea. Islay, Jura, Colonsay and Mull are within sight, but I am aware of the others spread out fan-wise in the ocean beyond.

It is a peaceful vision, but for me it is alive with memories of all the islanders that I have come to know during my time with Nàdair. It has been a huge privilege to work with these people, for whom environment, history and culture are inseparable from daily life. The communities of The Sea Kingdom may be remote, but they resonate with a collective determination to survive and thrive. In the words of Donald Black, Chairman of Comann Eachdraidh Lios Mòr:

> *'A community that has a knowledge of and an interest in its past will have the strength and courage to face the future.'*

Lead Partner Organisations & Projects

ARGYLL & BUTE COUNCIL MARINE & COASTAL DEVELOPMENT UNIT

Wildlife from the Boat
- Strategies for regional marine heritage protection, interpretation and visitor management developed and delivered.
- Leaflets & interpretation provided to help people identify and understand marine & island habitats and wildlife.

ARGYLL & THE ISLANDS ENTERPRISE

Heritage Tourism Training
- Heritage Tourism Training courses provided for 228 people. Topics included: Your Islands – Our Heritage, Tour Guide training, Wildlife Tourism Training, Working with Words, Family History, as well as study tours to the Western Isles and the Argyll Isles.

BUN OTHAN HARBOUR DEVELOPMENT AND RECREATION ASSOCIATION

Bun Othan Harbour
- 300 yards of path created, linking the two ends of Port Wemyss and providing picnic areas.
- Interpretation installed to highlight the history of this 1800's 'clearance village'.

BUTTERFLY CONSERVATION SCOTLAND

Butterflies and Burnet Moths: a Recovery Programme
- Management at butterfly and burnet moth sites in the islands improved by working closely with land managers.
- Training workshops on habitat management techniques provided for volunteers and countryside managers.
- 'Farmer-friendly' advice notes produced for three habitats/groups of species.
- Information leaflet about Argyll Islands Butterflies produced.

CO-CHOMANN DUALCHAS THIRIODH/ TIREE HERITAGE SOCIETY

Chapels & Pilgrimage Route, Tiree
- Two pre-reformation ruined chapels at Kirkapol stabilised and a wheelchair accessible path constructed to the site.
- Way-marked pilgrimage route created, linking the Kirkapol chapels to many other sites of Christian and Pre-Christian significance around the Island.
- Comprehensive guide book produced to accompany the route, describing the archaeological, ecclesiastical and natural heritage of Tiree.
- Nud's notebook published in English and Gaelic – a children's story book on the theme of Tiree's heritage and folklore.

Kilkenneth & St. Patrick's Chapels, Tiree
- Remains of two early Christian chapels (both scheduled monuments) preserved and interpreted.

COLL COMMUNITY LEARNING FORUM

The Flowers of Coll & Tiree and an Index to the Coll Magazine
- User-friendly full colour guide book to the flowers of Coll & Tiree produced.
- Digital version of all previous issues of the annual Coll Magazine (local history), made available on-line with a searchable index.

COLL PRESERVATION & WILDLIFE MANAGEMENT GROUP

Assessment of Predation on Breeding Waders
- Ground nesting birds protected from predation by trapping ferrets on the eastern side of Coll.
- Impact of predation on ground nesting wader success assessed through a comparative study of east & west Coll.

COMANN EACHDRAIDH LIOS MÒR

Tigh Iseabail Dhaidh, Lismore
- Former croft house on the Island of Lismore reconstructed to portray the life of the crofting community in the 19th century.

Ionad Naomh Moluag – Lismore Gaelic Heritage Museum
- Environmentally friendly museum constructed adjacent to Tigh Iseabail Dhaidh to house artefacts and displays illustrating the heritage of the Isle of Lismore.
- Facilities created for education in Gaelic and other aspects of cultural and natural heritage.
- Library, coffee shop and meeting space provided for the community and visitors.

COLONSAY COMMUNITY DEVELOPMENT COMPANY

Colonsay and Oronsay – A Wildlife and Heritage Guide
- Leaflet produced to introduce visitors to the Isle of Colonsay's rich and varied heritage.

Rhododendron Clearance Initiative
- Eradication programme for invasive Rhododendron ponticum implemented on Colonsay to restore and protect island biodiversity.

Improving Access to Sites of Archaeological Interest
- Key archaeological sites of interest to islanders and visitors identified.
- Ease of access to each site ensured by clearing vegetation.
- Detailed leaflet produced to promote access to and enjoyment and understanding of Colonsay's archaeological heritage.

CO-ROINN GHÀIDHLIG MHUILE AGUS IDHE/ MULL & IONA GAELIC PARTNERSHIP

Community Gaelic
◆ 'Gaelic Now!' CD produced to promote understanding of and access to Gaelic culture amongst locals and visitors.

CO-ROINN GHÀIDHLIG THIRIODH 'S CHOLLA/TIREE & COLL GAELIC PARTNERSHIP

An Iodhlann Archive
◆ New database for the archive's collection of over 9,000 items about the Island created, replacing time-consuming manual searches through the accession records.
◆ Series of detailed, largely bi-lingual Gaelic & English information sheets on Tiree habitats and species produced. Topics include seals, corncrakes, the kelp industry, brown hares, geese and machair.

An Iodhlann – A Virtual Archive
◆ On-line archive about Tiree created, enabling virtual visitors to see and hear 600 hand-picked 'crown jewels' from the collection, including a mixture of photographs, documents and sound clips.

DISCOVER COLL

Island Interpretation, Coll
◆ 'Discover Coll' leaflet produced, introducing visitors to the archaeology, geology, history and folklore of the Island and providing guidelines for safe and sensitive exploration of its landscapes.
◆ A series of talks about island heritage held for visitors.

FINLAGGAN TRUST

Finlaggan Development & Environmental Improvement
◆ Medieval chapel on Eilean Mòr in Loch Finlaggan, Isle of Islay, consolidated and carved grave slabs protected.

Nerabus Burial Ground and Carved Stones
◆ Carved stones dating from the time of the Lordship of the Isles conserved and protected near Port Charlotte on Islay.
◆ On-site interpretation and improvements to access installed.

Finlaggan Interpretation Hub
◆ New facility constructed to provide an interpretation centre relating to the Lordship of the Isles.

HEBRIDEAN WHALE AND DOLPHIN TRUST

Marine Education and Interpretation (2 projects)
Marine Outreach & Floating Classroom
Community Sealife Sightings Programme
Marine Biodiversity & Environmental Training

◆ 65ft yacht Silurian operated as a floating classroom around the isles with school groups coming aboard to take part in educational activities related to Argyll's marine environment.
◆ Marine education visits carried out by HWDT education staff to schools, preschool groups, Gaelic medium units and special needs groups throughout the Sea Kingdom.
◆ University level marine life courses developed and delivered.
◆ Workshops and training provided in marine conservation, sealife identification and marine awareness to marine users, students, island communities & volunteers.
◆ Marine Heritage booklets produced for Mull and Coll & Tiree.
◆ Sealife sighting programme established to gather and record information on cetaceans in Argyll coastal waters involving volunteers and schools.
◆ Marine cetacean surveys carried out with volunteer surveyors on board Silurian.
◆ Issues linked to the Local Biodiversity Action Plan for Argyll & Bute monitored & investigated. Internet link developed between schools and the HWDT research data resource.
◆ Marine environment project work for secondary school pupils supported with visits & field trips. Specialised courses in Marine Coastal Ecotourism delivered.
◆ Programme of public events and talks including 1st West Coast Whale Festival.
◆ Marine life Video produced & distributed. Marine life Website created and regular newsletters produced.

IONAD CHALUIM CHILLE ÌLE/ THE COLUMBA CENTRE ISLAY

Seanchas Ìle
◆ 'Seanchas' events held, where tradition-bearers shared their heritage with other islanders.
◆ Aspects of traditional Islay life in Gaelic, particularly the declining Islay dialect, preserved in text and sound.
◆ Texts, recordings and translations made available to the public in the Columba Centre, Bowmore, Islay.
◆ Book and CD of the project produced.

ISLAY DEVELOPMENT COMPANY

'Discover Islay & Jura' Leaflet
◆ Brochure produced to promote and raise awareness of the Island of Islay, the island's language and its rich and varied heritage, culture and environment.

Woollen Mill Renovation and Workshop
◆ Grade 1 Listed Waulkmill at Islay Woollen Mill restored for use as a weaving demonstration, training and interpretation venue.

ISLAY DEVELOPMENT COMPANY/ISLAY HEALTHY LIVING/ISLAY COMMUNITY ACCESS GROUP

Islay Community Access Development Phase 1 & 2
◆ Community-based access strategy developed for Islay's countryside.
◆ Over 20 walking routes established, including provision of stiles, path surfacing, way-markers interpretation and car parking.
◆ Promotional materials developed including an Explore Islay leaflet.
◆ Regular walking groups established in association with Paths to Health.

Balephetrish Bay – Isle of Tiree

Lismore lighthouse

ISLE OF GIGHA HERITAGE TRUST

Achamore Gardens

◆ 3-year development programme to renovate a world class garden and plant collection and promote increased visitor numbers.

◆ Skills developed through volunteer programmes and staff training to ensure continuity of specialist skills & knowledge.

ISLE OF JURA DEVELOPMENT TRUST

Jura Heritage, Access & Interpretation

◆ Interpretation boards, brochures, signage and on-line information provided for visitors.

◆ Access at the north end of the island, close to the Corrievreckan whirlpool, improved with the restoration of Kinuachdrachd pier.

ISLE OF LUING COMMUNITY TRUST

Heritage Interpretation

◆ Interpretative panels provided relating to the natural and cultural history of this historic slate quarrying and cattle breeding island.

◆ Benches and picnic tables.

◆ Walk leaflets.

MULL HISTORICAL & ARCHAEOLOGICAL SOCIETY

Consolidation of Moy Castle

◆ Upper levels of Moy Castle (c. 1400) consolidated to forestall imminent collapse.

◆ Associated archaeology investigated and recorded.

◆ Interpretation provided on site telling the story of the Clan McLaine, the castle and its later role in the iconic wartime film 'I Know Where I'm Going'.

Isle of Mull On-Line Museum

New website developed to:

◆ Promote the historical attractions of Mull.

◆ Provide a research resource with cross referenced data search facility.

◆ Make available material digitised from tape recordings, film & images.

◆ Provide a genealogical database linking to other islands.

◆ Provide a shop window for sales & marketing related to Mull's heritage.

MULL & IONA COMMUNITY TRUST

Mull & Iona Wildlife & Heritage Trail

◆ Island heritage trail created around Mull, including ten car parks and view points, to improve accessibility at key locations and reduce impacts on sensitive sites.

◆ Wildlife and Heritage Trail leaflet produced providing information on the Island's wildlife, geological, archaeological and environmental heritage.

Argyll Islands Native Woodland Project

◆ Programme of events held to raise awareness of the recreational, heritage, productivity and socio-economic benefits of woodlands.

◆ Suitable woodland expansion areas on Mull identified through ecological modelling, site assessment and community consultation.

ORONSAY LTD

Celtic Priory, Oronsay

◆ Priority areas of the fabric of an important 14th–16th Century priory on the Isle of Oronsay consolidated.

ROSS OF MULL HISTORICAL CENTRE

Discover the Ross

◆ Seven way-marked walking trails developed on the Ross of Mull.

◆ Full-colour guide books produced for the walking trails, telling the story of the area and interpreting its social, cultural, built, geological and archaeological heritage.

Tigh an Rois

◆ Museum created in a converted cottage in the village of Bunessan exhibiting heritage artefacts alongside photographic, written and interactive displays.

◆ Open air heritage exhibition established around the Old Corn Mill in Bunessan on the theme of 'Land to Mouth'.

◆ Archive of culture and family history in the Ross of Mull developed, including oral history, digitised documents and related materials.

◆ Social events held engaging islanders and visitors in local traditions & culture.

ROYAL SOCIETY FOR THE PROTECTION OF BIRDS (RSPB) SCOTLAND

Schools Heritage

◆ Topic boxes covering 4 different themes – Living on my Island, Freshwater, Island Species, The Sea – distributed to all 18 primary schools in the Argyll Atlantic Islands. Sustainable Development topic box distributed to all 5 secondary schools in the region, along with training and support for teachers.

Corncrake & Chough Recovery (2 projects)

◆ Island farmers supported to adopt corncrake and chough friendly land management practises.
◆ Range of potential nest sites for choughs enhanced on Islay.
◆ Site monitoring of species carried out.

Land and Countryside Management (10 projects)

At Totronald Reserve, Loch Gruinart Reserve, Smaull Farm and Mull of Oa on Islay, Oronsay Reserve and The Reef on Tiree:
◆ Land management to maintain and enhance corncrake populations.
◆ Livestock management to enhance chough habitats.
◆ Implementation of traditional Hebridean arable rotation systems to benefit farmland birds.
◆ Conservation and enhancement wetlands to increase numbers of breeding waders, botanical diversity and wintering geese.
◆ Conservation of dunes & machair through appropriate grazing systems.
◆ Restoration of previously drained blanket bog.
◆ Conservation and enhancement of marsh fritillary and northern mining bee habitat.
◆ Provision and upgrade of visitor access and interpretation facilities.
◆ Programme of visits and guided walks.

Operation Easter – Sea Eagle Watch

◆ 24hr volunteer watch mounted to prevent nest robberies and disturbance to sea eagles at the critical egg stage.
◆ Equipment provided to community volunteers engaged in the eagle watch.
◆ Remote and direct viewing facilities provided to allow volunteers and visitors to view sea eagles in a well managed and informative environment.

Birds of Tiree & Coll Book

◆ Comprehensive guidebook describing the islands' birds produced, including local Gaelic species names and information on where and when to see birds and other wildlife on Tiree and Coll.

Wildlife for All

All schools in the Argyll Islands and associated coastal mainland provided with:
◆ a guide to exploring the wildlife of their island.
◆ a starter pack of identification guides.
◆ observation and viewing equipment linked to the needs/size of the school.
◆ access to partner specialists on the islands.

SCAPE TRUST & THE CENTRE FOR ENVIRONMENTAL HISTORY AND POLICY, ST. ANDREWS UNIVERSITY

Coastal Archaeology, Islay, Coll & Tiree

◆ Archaeological surveys carried out in the coastal zones of Islay, Coll & Tiree.
◆ Local 'shorewatch' groups established & trained to monitor sites and report on damage and erosion problems.

TIREE BUSINESS CENTRE

Tiree – A Wildlife and Heritage Guide

◆ Leaflet produced to provide information on wildlife, beaches, machair, archaeology, history and traditional crofting culture, with an emphasis on the relationship between man and environment which has shaped today's island landscape.

TIREE RURAL DEVELOPMENT LTD

Tiree Rural Development Plan

◆ Awareness of Tiree's crofting heritage promoted through interpretation and a programme of activities and events for islanders, children and visitors.
◆ Traditional crofting practices supported through a programme of training and development activities for island farmers.
◆ Island culture and economy supported through the operation of dedicated facilities at the Tiree Rural Centre.

'Water and Birds' Loch a' Phuill

◆ Hydrological study of an internationally important Special Protection Area carried out to investigate appropriate management actions to enhance habitat for breeding and wintering water birds and maintain public water supplies during dry summer periods.

TIREE WORKING GROUP

Loch Bhasapol Improvement, Tiree

◆ Works to regulate water levels and control bank erosion in an important wildlife habitat and recreation site.
◆ Loch zoning to delineate public-use and wildlife habitat areas.
◆ Provision of a parking area & interpretation.

VISITSCOTLAND

Heritage Leaflet and Promotions (2 projects)

◆ A comprehensive leaflet introducing visitors to the heritage of Scotland's Sea Kingdom in 6 languages produced and subsequently updated and reprinted.
◆ Eleven local Tourist Information Points refurbished on islands and at mainland ferry piers.
◆ Sea Kingdom website created.

Sea Kingdom Discovery Exhibition, Oban

◆ Exhibition created in the Oban Tourist Information Centre to showcase the Argyll Islands, featuring new film & audio material and capturing the built, natural and cultural heritage of the region.

Wind turbine – Gigha

Acknowledgements

FUNDERS

The following organisations contributed generous funding and in-kind support to the Nàdair 1 and 2 programmes between 2000 and 2008. The projects were also supported by donations made by hundreds of individual friends and supporters.

A special mention must be made of the Heritage Lottery Fund (HLF), the largest single contributor to the Nàdair programmes. Our thanks go to the staff at the HLF Edinburgh office and particularly to the two independent monitors appointed by HLF – David Hughes Hallett and Stewart Anderson – who gave invaluable support, advice and encouragement to Nàdair staff and project leaders throughout the programmes.

Thanks are also due to the staff of Oban Tourist Information Centre, home of the Nàdair office for eight years, for their good company and invaluable support.

Argyll & Bute Council ◆ Argyll Estates ◆ Argyll, the Isles, Loch Lomond, Stirling & Trossachs Tourist Board ◆ BBC Wildlife Charles Hayward Foundation ◆ Clan MacLean Heritage Trust ◆ Clan MacLean of Lochbuie ◆ Clothworkers Foundation Co-Chomann Dualchas Thiriodh ◆ Coll Magazine ◆ Colonsay Community Development Company Community Economic Development Programme ◆ Community Environmental Renewal Scheme Co-Roinn Ghàidhlig Thiriodh 's Cholla ◆ Crofters Commission ◆ Discover Coll ◆ Earthwatch ◆ Esmee Fairbairn Foundation Forest Enterprise ◆ Forestry Commission Scotland ◆ Forward Scotland ◆ Foster Yeoman Ltd. Gaelic in the Community (Gàidhlig sa Choimhearsnachd) ◆ Heritage Lottery Fund ◆ HIE Argyll and the Isles ◆ Historic Scotland Holiday Mull ◆ HWDT Staff, Committee and volunteers ◆ INTERREG IIIB – ISLA ◆ Islay Development Company ◆ Islay Estates Company Islay Natural Heritage Trust ◆ Kiloran Farms ◆ Leader + WHELK ◆ Lorne MacLaine of Lochbuie ◆ MacBackpackers Mrs F. Colburn ◆ Mull & Iona Community Trust ◆ Mull Historical & Archaeological Society ◆ National Trust for Scotland Ross of Mull Historical Centre ◆ Royal Society for the Protection of Birds (Scotland) ◆ Sandra Trust Scottish Executive Biodiversity Action Grants Scheme ◆ Scottish Government Rural Challenge Fund ◆ Scottish Land Fund Scottish Natural Heritage ◆ Scottish Rural Partnership Fund – Local Capital Grants Scheme ◆ Sealgair Trust ◆ The Project Trust Tiree Business Centre ◆ Tiree Working Group ◆ World Wildlife Fund

PROJECT PARTICIPANTS

Each one of the Nàdair projects depended on the hard work and dedication of committee members, volunteers and project workers, not to mention their partners and families. Many are named below, but inevitably some will have been missed. Our warmest thanks are due to all.

A MacCalman ◆ A Shaw ◆ Adam Dawson ◆ Aisa Nebreda ◆ Alan Hobbett ◆ Alan Leitch ◆ Alan McIlroy ◆ Alan Parker Alasdair MacKellar ◆ Alasdair MacLachlan ◆ Alasdair Robb ◆ Alasdair Sinclair ◆ Alastair Fleming ◆ Alastair MacLean ◆ Alec MacArthur Alex Dunnachie ◆ Alex MacLean ◆ Alice Lambert ◆ Alison Fraser ◆ Alison Gill ◆ Alison Robertson ◆ Alistair Lavery ◆ Amber Knight An Acarsaid, Coll ◆ An Iodhlann, Tiree ◆ Andrea Sayers ◆ Andrew Abrahams ◆ Andrew Cameron ◆ Andrew Livingstone Andrew Montgomery ◆ Andrew Saul ◆ Andrew Warmsley ◆ Andy Oliver ◆ Andy Tait ◆ Angela Yeoman ◆ Angus Kennedy ◆ Angus Keys Angus McKechnie ◆ Angus Munn ◆ Anja Lamont ◆ Ann Clark ◆ Ann Hughes ◆ Ann MacQueen ◆ Ann Steele ◆ Anna NicGhille Anne Baxter ◆ Anne Cleave ◆ Archie MacColl ◆ Archie MacGillivray ◆ Archie Sproat ◆ Argyll Estates ◆ Arinagour Primary School Attie MacKechnie ◆ Audrey Dickie ◆ Audrey Martin ◆ B and Kenneth Cassels ◆ Barbara Jones ◆ Barbara Weir ◆ Barry Edmundson Barry Wilson ◆ Ben Weaser ◆ Bernie Smith ◆ Bert Leitch ◆ Bill Lawson ◆ Birgit Whitmore ◆ Border Signs & Graphics ◆ Brian Heaton

ACKNOWLEDGEMENTS

Brian Milne ◆ Bryony MacFarlane ◆ Butterfly and Burnet Moths volunteers and participating land managers ◆ CADISPA ◆ Cally Fleming ◆ Carl Reavey ◆ Carol Muir ◆ Caroline Lathe ◆ Caroline Strachan ◆ Caroline Young ◆ Carolyn Brodie MacKay ◆ Catherine Gillies ◆ Cathie Carmichael ◆ Catriona Bell ◆ Catriona Craig ◆ Catriona MacLennan ◆ Catriona McLeod ◆ Catriona Young ◆ CELM & Taic CELM Board & Committee ◆ CELM volunteers ◆ Charlie Self ◆ Charlotte Hoad ◆ Chris Jones ◆ Chris Nisbet ◆ Chris Parsons ◆ Christa Byrne ◆ Christine Bannister ◆ Clare Hoare ◆ Clare Jones ◆ Claudia Ferguson-Smyth ◆ Clive McKay ◆ Colin and Hugh MacKinnon ◆ Colin Campbell ◆ Colin McFarlane ◆ Colin Smith ◆ Colin Woodcock, Blue Beyond ◆ Coll Community Council ◆ Colonsay Estate ◆ Colum Scott ◆ D Caldwell ◆ D J MacPhee ◆ D MacKenzie ◆ D McFadyen ◆ Dave Hannah ◆ David Bridges ◆ David Greenhalgh ◆ David Haworth ◆ David McDonald ◆ David Ritchie ◆ David Roberts ◆ David Sexton ◆ David Warnock ◆ David White ◆ David Woodhouse ◆ David Wyles ◆ Dawn MacKenzie ◆ Debbie Smyth ◆ Dee Rudiger ◆ Déirdre Ní Mhathúna ◆ Derek Bannister ◆ Diorbhail Dennis ◆ Dom Morgan ◆ Dòmhnall Angaidh MacIllinnein ◆ Dòmhnall MacPhaidein ◆ Donald Bell ◆ Donald Black ◆ Donald G Woodrow ◆ Donald J Campbell ◆ Donald MacIntyre ◆ Donald MacKinnon ◆ Donald MacLean ◆ Doug Young ◆ Douglas Carslaw ◆ Duncan Cameron ◆ Duncan Grant ◆ Duncan MacGregor ◆ Duncan MacLean ◆ Duncan MacLeod ◆ Duncan Strachan ◆ Eagle Watch Volunteers ◆ Edwina Proudfoot ◆ Elaine Campbell. ◆ Eleanor Logan ◆ Eleanor McNab ◆ Eleanor NicDugaill ◆ Emily Edwards ◆ Emma Grant ◆ Eoghann MacLachlan ◆ Ernie Green ◆ Fergus Younger ◆ Fieldfare Trust ◆ Fiona Cruickshanks ◆ Fiona Kennedy ◆ Fiona MacKinnon ◆ Fiona Quarmby ◆ Fiona Shannon ◆ Flora Lamont ◆ Frances MacIntyre ◆ Fraoch Nic an Deòir ◆ Freddie Everett ◆ Friends of Tiree Chapels ◆ Fumiko Miller ◆ Geoff Fagan & team ◆ George Lyon MSP ◆ Georgina Hobhouse ◆ Gillian Rae ◆ Gina McAuslin ◆ Gordon Covell ◆ Graham Kent ◆ H. MacKinnon ◆ Hilda Bransby ◆ Hubert Saldanha ◆ Hugh and Linda Boa ◆ Hugh MacQueen ◆ Hugh McPhee ◆ HWDT committee and volunteers ◆ Iain Howell ◆ Iain MacKinnon ◆ Iain Milligan ◆ Ian Campbell ◆ Ian Cruickshanks ◆ Ian Downie ◆ Ian MacFadyen ◆ Islay Community Access Group committee and volunteers ◆ J McGilvary ◆ J McKay ◆ Jack Fleming ◆ Jacqueline Hoey ◆ Jacqui McLeod ◆ James Farren ◆ James How ◆ James MacCormick ◆ James McKeand ◆ Jamie Spiers ◆ Jan Dunlop ◆ Jane Dawson ◆ Jane Dodd ◆ Jane Isaacson ◆ Jane MacLachlan ◆ Jane Rose ◆ Janet Hunter Bowler ◆ Janet MacDonald ◆ Jennifer Baker ◆ Jenny Smith ◆ Jim Corbett ◆ Jim Hill ◆ Jim Houchen ◆ Jim McLoughlin ◆ Joan Morgan ◆ Joanna Wright ◆ John Bowler ◆ John Busby ◆ John Cable ◆ John Cameron ◆ John Fraser ◆ John Holliday ◆ John McGhie ◆ John Morgan ◆ John Roberston ◆ John Smith ◆ Johnny Johnston ◆ Josie Brown ◆ Julia Galbraith ◆ Julian Hill ◆ Julianna Nicholls ◆ Julie Williams ◆ Juliette Shrimpton ◆ June Watson ◆ Jura Development Trust Board of Directors ◆ Katie England ◆ Kaz Bailey ◆ Keith Gillon ◆ Keith Miller ◆ Kevin Byrne ◆ Kirsty Walker ◆ Lachie MacFadyen ◆ Lasta King ◆ Laura Mandelberg ◆ Laurie Campbell ◆ Lawrence Hilder ◆ Len Powell ◆ Lindy MacLellan ◆ Lismore Community ◆ Liz Lapsley ◆ Liz McLachlan ◆ Lorna Andrew ◆ Lorna Elliot ◆ Lorne Gill ◆ Louise Gregory ◆ Louise Walsh ◆ Lucy Hamilton ◆ Luing Primary ◆ Lynda MacCallum ◆ Lynn Vesco ◆ Lynne Farrell ◆ Maggie Campbell. ◆ Mairead NicEacharna ◆ Mairi Campbell ◆ Mairi Hedderwick ◆ Mairi MacKinnon ◆ Màiri NicGhilleMhìcheil ◆ Malcolm McNeill ◆ Malcolm Ogilvie ◆ Malcolm T Anderson ◆ Malcolm Younger ◆ Margaret F Anderson ◆ Margaret Heads ◆ Margaret King ◆ Margaret MacDonald ◆ Marij Van Helmond ◆ Marina Curran-Colthart ◆ Mark Vale ◆ Martin Hadlington ◆ Martin Whitmore ◆ Mary Ann MacInnes ◆ Mary Simpson ◆ Mat Louise MacQuarrie ◆ Mathew Steele ◆ Matt Doyle ◆ May Laird ◆ May MacCallum ◆ Meg Douglass ◆ MH & AS Committee ◆ Michael Fothergill ◆ Michael MacRae ◆ Mike Yendell ◆ Micky Little ◆ Mike Barlow ◆ Mike Peacock ◆ Mike Richardson ◆ Mrs Betsy West ◆ Mull Historical & Archaeological Society ◆ Nan Shaw ◆ Nancy Fettes ◆ Neil Cameron ◆ Neil MacCallum ◆ Neil MacCormick MEP ◆ Neil MacKinnon ◆ Nic Davies ◆ Nick Richardson ◆ Nicole Freire ◆ Nigel Grant ◆ Noelle Campbell ◆ Norman Bissell ◆ Norman Garnett ◆ Norman Storie ◆ Tom Morgan ◆ Oronsay Ltd. ◆ Pam Baker ◆ Pat Campbell ◆ Paul Daw ◆ Paul Green ◆ Paul Kirkland ◆ Peggy Nicholson ◆ Pete Hooper ◆ Peter Cool ◆ Peter Corbett ◆ Peter Hall ◆ Peter Ling ◆ Peter MacKay ◆ Peter Stevick ◆ Phil Johnstone ◆ Phil Robertson ◆ Project Trust, Coll ◆ Rae McKenzie ◆ Ray Michie MP ◆ Residents of Gigha ◆ Richard Demery ◆ Richard Evans ◆ Richard Henderson ◆ Rob Jones ◆ Rob Wainwright ◆ Robert Benn ◆ Robert Higham ◆ Robin Harvey ◆ Roger Broad ◆ Rona MacKenzie ◆ Ronnie Campbell ◆ Ros Jones ◆ Rosie Burgess ◆ Ross Lilley ◆ Rosy Barlow ◆ Ruth Sturgeon ◆ Sally Ling ◆ Sandy MacCallum ◆ Sandy Shairp ◆ Sarah Barry ◆ Sarah Benfield ◆ Sarah Money ◆ Sarah Rose ◆ SCAPE ◆ Selkie Associates ◆ Seumas Westland ◆ Shane Cadzow ◆ Shauna Cameron ◆ Shona McConnell ◆ Shorewatch Volunteers ◆ Sid Bowman ◆ Simon Blackett ◆ Simon Breasley ◆ Simon Wellock ◆ Sophie Isaacson ◆ Steve Pardue ◆ Steve Thomson ◆ Steve Walton ◆ Steven Dott ◆ Steven Raw ◆ Stewart MacDougall ◆ Stuart Carmichael ◆ Sue Boocock ◆ Sue Fink ◆ Sue Hooper ◆ Sue Scott ◆ Susan Allan ◆ Susan Chisholm ◆ Susan Lamont ◆ Susie Barrett ◆ Susie Chalupa ◆ Suzanne & Bill Patterson ◆ Tania Hunter ◆ Terry Donovan ◆ Tim Lister ◆ Timothy Laing ◆ Tom Dawson ◆ Tom Gaillard ◆ Tom Marshall ◆ Tom Prescott ◆ Tony Baker ◆ Tony Oliver ◆ Tony Perkins ◆ Tracy Little ◆ Tristan ap Rheinallt ◆ Ulrike Johnson ◆ Val Conway ◆ Val Peacock ◆ Wendy Castle ◆ William MacLean ◆ Willie MacSporran ◆ Willie-Angus MacLean ◆ Yvonne Huntly ◆ Zoë Fleming ◆ Marjorie Adam ◆ Sue Watt ◆ Gavin McCall ◆ Paul Walton ◆ John Ward

NÀDAIR BOARD & STEERING GROUP

Chair
Patricia Bradley (2000–02 & 2005–06) ◆ Derek MacAdam (2002–05) ◆ Michael J. Robertson (2006–)

Directors
Alan McKie ◆ Alice Lambert ◆ Anthony Perkins ◆ Cally Fleming ◆ Catriona MacLennan ◆ Derek MacAdam ◆ Dorothy Breckenridge Dugie Bannatyne ◆ Elaine Robertson ◆ Eleanor Logan ◆ Georgina Hobhouse ◆ Ian Gillies ◆ James Fraser ◆ James Hilder ◆ Janette MacKay Joan Inglis ◆ John Findlay ◆ John Matthews ◆ Len Scoullar ◆ Mark Jennison ◆ Michael MacRae ◆ Mike Robertson ◆ Patricia Bradley

Steering Group
Andrew Campbell ◆ Ann MacSween ◆ Aonghus Mackechnie ◆ Bill Taylor ◆ Diane MacLeod ◆ Ian Close ◆ Jane Fowler ◆ John Raven John Ward ◆ Kevin Williams ◆ Lynne Farrell ◆ Mike Robinson ◆ Noel Fojut ◆ Rhona Sutherland ◆ Roddy Fairley

NÀDAIR STAFF

Gavin McColl (Project Manager 2000–2001) ◆ Dugie Bannatyne (Project Manager 2001–05/ Development Director 2005–06)
Craig Whyte (Project Officer 2001–2003) ◆ Caroline MacInnes (Project Administrator 2001–04)
Eleanor Shaw (Garty) (Project/ Senior Project Officer 2003–05/ General Manager 2005–07) ◆ Fiona Shannon (Project Administrator 2004)
Donna Ferguson (Project/ Senior Project Officer 2003–2007) ◆ Maggie Brotherston (Project Administrator 2005)
Nicola Welsh (Project/ Senior Project Officer 2006–2008) ◆ Mary MacGregor (Project/ Senior Project Officer 2007–2008)
Carlo Beuger (Chief Executive 2007–2008) ◆ Morag MacNeil (Project Officer 2007) ◆ Ann MacLean (Project/ Senior Project Officer 2007–2008)
Neil Waslidge (Project Officer 2008)

Author's Note

My personal thanks go to every person named in the lists above, but I would like to give
particular recognition to Dugie Bannatyne, who set the course for all who came after,
Donna Ferguson, friend and longest-standing fellow worker, Nicola Welsh and Mary MacGregor,
who kept the flag flying, and Tony Perkins, who made it all worthwhile.

ELEANOR GARTY

*Eleanor Garty worked for the Nàdair Trust between 2003 and 2007. In this book she brings
together visits and conversations which took place over the course of four years and imagines them
into one very personal voyage around the Argyll Islands.*

South Beach – Coll